Building Wealth Through Property in Australia

BY

ROMEO CAPORASO

TABLE OF CONTENTS

BIOGRAPHY OF ROMEO CAPORASO

In 2022, while property markets in Sydney and Melbourne stagnated, Adelaide property values surged 25%. In 2024, they climbed another 15%. If you missed those opportunities, don't worry. The next wave is building, and this book will show you exactly how to catch it.

My name is Romeo Caporaso, and over the past 25 years, I've helped hundreds of South Australians build substantial wealth through strategic property investment. More importantly, I've done it myself...

I will share with you my knowledge that helps you profit from my experience fast. The knowledge guiding you in this book comes from over fifteen years of experience as a tax agent, having personally developed properties, bought and built multiple properties, worked in the Australian Tax Office, and witnessed more successful property transactions through my accounting practice.

Romeo Caporaso was born and raised in Adelaide to Italian migrant parents. He enjoyed finishing school at just 16 and university at 19. After completing university in 1992, he began his career in Business Banking at Commonwealth Bank, working in both Adelaide and Sydney's

Eastern suburbs. A notable achievement during his time in Sydney was purchasing his first property in Hurstville at the age of 23.

Returning to Adelaide, Romeo held accounting roles at RAA Insurance and Rossdale Homes, where he notably implemented the newly introduced Goods and Services Tax. He also worked for the Australian Taxation Office.

Romeo eventually transitioned from being an employee to self-employment, starting businesses in personal training, bookkeeping, and website services. In 2010, he achieved his goal of becoming a tax agent and focused on building his accounting practice. Starting with no clients, no staff, and working from home, his business has grown significantly. By 2013, it became Xero-certified and an early adopter of online accounting. More recently, achieving Xero Gold partner status and issued over $5 million in invoices through

Xero. The business now operates from dedicated premises with a small team of staff members.

His accounting practice has supported hundreds of businesses in modern accounting compliance and growth, and has launched dozens of accountants into their careers through employment and internships. A key development was transitioning from the number crunching days of MYOB in 2005 to a paperless, technology and consultative-driven accounting system.

Romeo's business has also facilitated the commencement of over a hundred Super Funds (SMSFs) and wealth-building for retirement. He personally owns an SMSF that holds property and shares. He advocates for building more than $1 million in superannuation by retirement.

As an experienced investment property owner, Romeo built his own home and recently completed a property development project by transforming his parents' home into townhouses. This project significantly enriched his expertise in accounting and property development. He specializes in property tax, property development, construction businesses, trade businesses, and investment properties.

Romeo practices what he preaches, achieving success in business, property, and superannuation.

Meet Romeo, phone us on 08 8337 4460 to come in for a coffee and chat. Find out more about Tax Accounting Adelaide and schedule a meeting. He can help you get underway with your property wealth building.

Book in for your property tax advice session at https://bit.ly/4oNQ5Nb. More information at Property Accountant Adelaide | Tax Accounting Adelaide or Expert tax Adelaide | Tax Accounting Adelaide.

INTRODUCTION

Property changed my life more than wages ever did. I saw that early in my career. I worked in banking and later as an accountant. I helped people with taxes and business. The real turning point came when I started buying my own properties and saw how capital growth-built wealth in the background.

This book shares what I learned from that journey. I grew up in Adelaide, and I have worked with hundreds of clients across Australia. I have seen how ordinary earners use property to grow their net worth. I have also seen how some people missed out because they waited too long or sold too early.

You will see why Australian residential property has stayed strong over time. I explain how markets like Adelaide have grown in recent years and why demand and limited supply keep pushing prices higher. I also show how tax rules such as negative gearing and the main residence exemption can support your strategy when you structure things well.

The chapters guide you from "why property" to "how to buy" in a clear way. You will learn how to think about capital growth and rental income. You will see example numbers and simple scenarios. You will also see how small actions, such as getting a depreciation report or choosing the right loan, can increase your tax refunds and improve your cash flow.

This is not a book about quick flips. It is about buying quality property and holding it for many years. I explain why selling too soon often becomes the biggest regret. I show how time, compounding growth, and forced saving through your mortgage can do the heavy lifting. I also talk about risk. You will read about job loss, interest rate changes, relationship breakdowns, and other issues that can threaten your plans and how to prepare for them.

You will also find a step-by-step path for your first or next purchase. I walk you through borrowing capacity, pre-approval, working with agents, using a conveyancer, and setting up your tax records. I show you how to use equity and how to think about deposits, lender's mortgage insurance, and new government schemes that reduce the deposit hurdle.

My aim is simple. I want you to see property as a practical tool. I want you to understand why it works in Australia and how to use it with confidence. If you are willing to learn and to act, then you can let your own "investment tree" grow and see where it takes you.

This is a property investment book written specifically for Australian investors by a local tax expert who's actually done it himself.

Welcome to Building Wealth Through Property in Australia, a comprehensive guide designed to help you navigate the dynamic and rewarding world of property investment in Australia. Whether you're a first-time buyer, seasoned investor, or simply exploring the idea of property ownership, this book provides valuable insights, strategies, and practical advice to help you make informed decisions and achieve your financial goals.

Australia's property market has long been considered one of the most stable and lucrative investment opportunities globally. With consistent capital growth, strong rental demand, and favourable tax advantages, property investment remains a cornerstone of wealth creation for many Australians. However, the journey to successful property ownership requires careful planning, research, and professional guidance.

In this guide, you'll find detailed information on the benefits of property investment, recent market trends, and the key factors driving property values in cities like Adelaide, Sydney, Melbourne, and beyond. You'll also learn about the importance of long-term investment strategies, tax optimization, and risk management to ensure sustainable success in property ownership.

The author, Romeo Caporaso, brings decades of experience in accounting, property development, and investment to this book. His expertise in property tax, wealth-building strategies, and modern accounting practices has helped hundreds of Australians achieve financial freedom through property investment. Romeo's personal journey, from purchasing his first property at 23 to building a successful accounting practice and completing property development projects, serves as a testament to the transformative power of property investment.

This guide is packed with actionable tips, case studies, and step-by-step instructions to help you take the first step toward building your property portfolio. Whether you're looking to buy your first home, invest in rental properties, or explore advanced strategies like property development or

Self-Managed Super Fund (SMSF), this book is your roadmap to success.

As you embark on your property investment journey, I often say that, like the fruit tree, the best time to invest in property was ten years ago, but the second-best time is now. Let this guide inspire and empower you to take action, make smart decisions, and create lasting wealth through property investment in Australia.

REASONS TO INVEST IN PROPERTY

RECENT PROPERTY MARKET PERFORMANCE

Recent Property Market Values Explained.

Here are some recent property increase indicators.

It is notable that after property stagnation for many years, Adelaide's property market grew 25% in 2022 and 15% in 2024.

CoreLogic daily home value index

31 October 2024

CITY - ALL DWELLINGS	CHANGE DAY ON DAY	TODAY'S VALUE	% CHANGE QTR ON QTR	% CHANGE YR ON YR
Sydney	0.06 ^	238.5	0.2%	3.7%
Melbourne	0.14 ^	179	-0.7%	-2%
Brisbane*	0.07 ^	194.5	2.3%	12.9%
Adelaide	0.09 ^	205.1	3.7%	15%
Perth	0.04 ^	172.4	4.5%	25.3%
5 capital city aggregate	0.03 ^	205.1	1.1%	6.3%

Here's some data from CoreLogic, reflecting annual changes to major cities' property values for the past year.

Median house prices and annual percentage change, March quarter 2022

Capital city	March Qtr 2021 - 2022 Annual change (%)	March Qtr 2022 Median house price ($)	Regional (a)	March Qtr 2021 - 2022 Annual change (%)	March Qtr 2022 Median house price ($)
Sydney	16.4	1,245,000	New South Wales	29.1	800,300
Melbourne	9.4	930,000	Victoria	17.4	640,000
Brisbane	29.3	787,500	Queensland	12.8	530,000
Adelaide	23.8	650,000	South Australia	18.7	362,000
Perth	1.9	550,000	Western Australia	4.9	425,000
Hobart	23.4	753,000	Tasmania	30.0	520,000
Darwin	12.1	600,000	Northern Territory	2.4	461,000
Canberra	28.3	1,065,000			

Here are some more growth figures from 2022 from the
Australian Bureau of Statistics.

Adelaide Median Property Prices

Adelaide's median property price

Here is the latest data on the median property prices for Adelaide.

Property	Median price Δ	MoM Δ	QoQ Δ	Annual Δ
All Capital city dwellings	$808,644	1.1%	3.7%	15.0%
Capital city houses	$864,487	1.0%	3.6%	14.5%
Capital city units	$574,362	1.7%	4.2%	18.5%
Regional dwellings	$440,599	1.3%	3.0%	11.3%

Source: CoreLogic, 1st November 2024

The Adelaide property market remains one of the countries top performing markets rising for the seventh consecutive quarter.

The pace of growth remains high and well above the historical average as low stock levels intensify competition.

The comparative affordability of the city's homes has seen prices defy the significant increase in interest rates since May 2022, but this affordability gap is now disappearing.

CoreLogic data shows Adelaide values recorded a COVID-19 "trough to peak" growth of 70.8 per cent.

Like in most capital cities, low stock levels are also helping to insulate home values, with increased competition among potential buyers

The strong auction clearance rates are an indication of the depth of the Adelaide property market and while they started a little lower this year, the depth of buyer demand has kept Adelaide auction clearance rates high.

Latest Market Updates

Adelaide's property market has shown steady growth in 2025, continuing its strong performance from previous years. As of February 2025, the median dwelling price in Adelaide was $822,201, reflecting an annual increase of 11.9%. Houses specifically saw 11.5% annual growth, with a median price of $873,029.

By March 2025, the market remained resilient, with house values increasing by 10.6% annually and unit values rising by 13.9% per annum. The median dwelling value reached $827,675, supported by strong buyer demand and a reduction in the official cash rate.

As of April 2025, Adelaide's median dwelling value was $825,776, with annual growth of 9.8%. The total return on property (capital growth + rent) stood at 13.7%, making Adelaide one of the strongest-performing markets in Australia.

By June 2025, the Adelaide property market recorded a median dwelling value of $829,400, representing 9.5% annual growth. Units in particular have remained in high demand, with affordability relative to houses pushing more buyers toward apartments and townhouses. Rental demand has surged, with gross rental yields rising to an average of 4.1% across Adelaide, among the highest of any capital city. Vacancy rates remain at historic lows of around 0.6%, adding further upward pressure on rents.

Overall, Adelaide's property market has remained robust, driven by limited supply, strong demand, and favourable economic conditions. Compared to Sydney and Melbourne,

Adelaide continues to attract interstate investors due to lower entry prices, consistent growth, and strong rental returns.

Staying Informed on Market Trends

This data may quickly become out of date, so it may be worthwhile to do your own current research. But the point of this data is to show you that property prices have been escalating in Australia over recent years.

Where it will go from here is a great question. It is important to keep up with the latest trends in property. A great source is the CoreLogic Home Value Index, along with reports from the Reserve Bank of Australia and local government planning updates.

In 2025, many analysts suggest that while national growth is moderating, Adelaide, Brisbane, and Perth are likely to continue outperforming the market due to affordability advantages, interstate migration, and strong rental markets. Sydney and Melbourne remain highly liquid markets, but affordability constraints mean growth rates may slow relative to smaller capitals.

Summary:

Capital city housing markets experienced price growth in October 2025, driven by the spring selling season, lower interest rates, and strong buyer and seller confidence. All capitals reported house price increases, with Darwin leading the monthly growth at 3.3%, followed by Adelaide (2.2%) and Brisbane (2.1%). Over the past year, Darwin, Brisbane, and Perth recorded the highest annual house price growth at 18.7%, 13.0%, and 11.3%, respectively.

Unit prices also rose nationally for the ninth consecutive month, up 1.0% in October. Brisbane led monthly unit price growth at 3.2%, followed by Melbourne (2.0%) and Adelaide (1.6%). Annual unit price growth was highest in Brisbane (19.7%), Adelaide (13.9%), and Perth (12.4%).

The housing market is supported by lower interest rates, a strong economy, low unemployment, and high migration levels, which contribute to housing undersupply, low rental vacancy rates, and rising rents. Government initiatives for First-Home Buyers are expected to further boost demand and prices. National home prices are projected to record strong growth in 2025, surpassing the previous two years.

Tabulated Data:

House Prices (October 2025)

City	Median Price	Monthly Growth	Annual Growth	1-Year Growth
Sydney	$1,763,774	1.2%	7.4%	7.4%
Melbourne	$1,114,604	1.5%	6.9%	6.0%
Brisbane	$1,124,113	2.1%	11.5%	13.0%
Adelaide	$1,063,334	2.2%	9.4%	9.0%
Perth	$1,055,554	1.6%	8.3%	11.3%
Hobart	$712,940	1.5%	7.0%	3.6%
Darwin	$744,679	3.3%	20.9%	18.7%
Canberra	$1,010,580	1.2%	9.2%	6.4%
National	$1,253,522	1.6%	8.2%	8.3%

Unit Prices (October 2025)

City	Median Price	Monthly Growth	Annual Growth	1-Year Growth
Sydney	$806,595	0.3%	4.7%	3.8%
Melbourne	$596,330	2.0%	8.4%	5.1%
Brisbane	$671,203	3.2%	14.5%	19.7%
Adelaide	$596,248	1.6%	11.5%	13.9%
Perth	$576,519	0.2%	10.7%	12.4%
Hobart	$536,590	-1.0%	-4.5%	9.0%
Darwin	$383,087	0.1%	8.6%	7.4%
Canberra	$500,132	-1.3%	-0.5%	0.6%
National	$703,409	1.0%	6.8%	6.3%

Key Insights:

1. **Top Performers (Monthly Growth):**

    o **Houses:** Darwin (3.3%), Adelaide (2.2%), Brisbane (2.1%).

    o **Units:** Brisbane (3.2%), Melbourne (2.0%), Adelaide (1.6%).

2. **Top Performers (Annual Growth):**

    o **Houses:** Darwin (18.7%), Brisbane (13.0%), Perth (11.3%).

    o **Units:** Brisbane (19.7%), Adelaide (13.9%), Perth (12.4%).

3. **Market Drivers:** Lower interest rates, strong economy, housing undersupply, and government initiatives for First-Home Buyers.

4. **Outlook:** Continued price growth expected in 2025, with Brisbane, Adelaide, and Perth leading the market.

THE VALUE OF TIME SPENT ON INVESTMENT PROPERTY

Time Commitments Required for Property Investment

Let's say you look for a property and you undertake all sorts of activities in buying a property. These may include time taken to see accountants, see property agents, inspect sites, gain bank approvals, maintain the property by your team, such as the agent or contractors, bookkeep some annual figures, keep those records, do tax returns, do inspections, liaise with property agents, and other activities such as some maintenance and administration.

In 2025, with digital tools, much of this process has become easier; online property inspections, digital conveyancing, and automated bookkeeping software now save investors significant time compared to a decade ago. However, demand for personal involvement in decision-making and property management still requires meaningful time commitments.

Why The Return on Time Is Remarkably High

To illustrate, let's say you spend 100 hours of your valuable lifetime doing this work toward investing in a property.

But let's say you bought a property that was conservatively appreciated from $500,000 to $700,000 over 20 years.

That would mean that the time you spent on making this profit would be around $200,000 divided by your 100 hours.

Which comes to $2000 per hour.

So, would you think that this time was well worth it? I'm sure you would agree, yes.

Otherwise, you could ask yourself, when are you ever paid that much per hour? How does this stack up to the top professional income rates? Pretty good, don't you think?

The truth is that many of us are not paid this well in our jobs or business in terms of return per hour.

In my experience as an accountant, this is one of the best ways to earn the most money for your time possible. And with Adelaide's property values rising nearly 10% annually in recent years, investors are seeing returns on time spent far above average wage growth, making property one of the most leveraged uses of personal time and resources.

KEY DRIVERS BEHIND ADELAIDE'S RISING PROPERTY VALUES

While Adelaide property may be considered relatively affordable compared to the national median and properties of other cities, there have been considerable property value increases. In general, there are factors contributing to increased demand and decreased supply of property in Adelaide.

Some of these factors include:

- Lack of trades contributing to slow building times.
- Infrastructure challenges, such as water connections.
- Lack of land and land releases, generally, no new land is available east and west of the city. Most new land releases are limited to the outer southern and northern areas of Adelaide.
- General lack of supply of property available.
- Average build times have increased from less than 12 months and have reached, in some circumstances, up to three years.
- Slower building times and difficulty in finding land mean to construct homes, favouring the less option of buying established homes, increasing demand for established residential properties. Building has additional risks such as delays from material and labour challenges, difficulty in having additional costs to budget without an available property residence, building disputes, and unplanned additional costs or errors, building stealing and pilfering until construction completion.
- The land value increases have squeezed down the profitability of smaller dwelling developments of

less than six dwellings. Unless you already own land, buying land at such premium rates makes it difficult to buy land, construct, and sell quickly for significant profit. Rather than quick selling, property developers may be forced to hold longer to make real estate profits.

- Obstructive tree regulations.
- Rising building labour and material costs, such as in timber and steel.
- Heritage protection areas hindering growth.
- Flood and fire-prone areas also limit land access.
- High migration growth demanding housing.
- New government rules, such as higher land size per dwelling, which is a minimum of 250 square meters per dwelling. Previous state and council relations allowed dwelling on smaller land sizes of around 150 square meters per dwelling.
- Increasing interest rates and cost of living.
- South Australia and other states are offering generous first home ownership incentives, including grants and stamp duty exemptions for dwellings of up to around $1 million, boosting demand further.
- The federal Government has also announced First-Home Buyers can buy homes up to $1 million with only a 5% deposit, which is to be distributed through the banking system. This is likely to generate further demand for property.

So, what does this mean? Perhaps even though prices are escalating, it seems they will continue to escalate in markets such as Adelaide and others, too.

The Sydney property market is always high and at a premium to other cities.

Melbourne property increases have been the most sluggish perhaps of any major city, but it too may be due for perhaps the highest increases in the short-term, as it is predicted to be a cheaper property market that property buyers will seek out.

THE IMPORTANCE OF LONG-TERM PROPERTY INVESTMENT

The Costs of Buying and Selling Property

Buying and selling property in Australia involves several costs that you should be aware of.

It is important to know about these. Also, to appreciate that they are all part of the investment journey in creating wealth in property. They are not a waste of money, but of course, it is important to obtain all these services at a good value and with great providers. This can make your property investment even more successful.

Here's a breakdown of the main expenses:

Buying a Property

1. **Purchase Price**: The largest cost, typically financed through savings and a mortgage.

2. **Stamp Duty**: A state tax that varies by state and property price. We recommend researching these costs on each state body's website or consulting your conveyancer.

3. **Conveyancer or Solicitor Fees:** These professionals handle the legal aspects of the transaction, costing between $900 and $2,200.

4. **Building and Pest Inspections:** Essential for assessing the property's condition, costing a few hundred dollars each.

5. **Lenders Mortgage Insurance (LMI)**: Required if

your deposit is less than 20% of the property's value.

6. **Loan Application Fees:** Covering the costs of setting up the mortgage, usually a few hundred dollars.

7. **Other Fees:** Including loan repayment fees, interest, and possibly a buyer's agent fee if you use one.

Selling a Property

1. **Real Estate Agent Fees:** Typically, 1-3% of the sale price, but can vary.

2. **Marketing Costs**: For advertising the property, ranging from $1,000 to $10,000, depending on the marketing strategy.

3. **Conveyancer or Solicitor Fees:** Like buying this service ensures you sell the property for the vendor, these fees range from $900 to $2,200.

4. **Lender Fees:** If you have a mortgage, you may need to pay discharge or early exit fees, usually between $150 and $1,500.

5. **Home Staging:** Optional but can enhance the property's appeal, costing up to $10,000. I think this is a great idea; rather than selling an empty property, potential buyers will have their imagination encouraged by seeing the property demonstrated in a better light and full of wonderful decorations.

These costs can add up, so it's important to budget accordingly.

Why Holding Property Long-Term Makes Sense

Given that there are substantial costs in buying and selling properties. I believe it's best to hold them as long as possible.

Getting in and out of properties in a short time frame will barely give you a chance to recoup the buying and selling costs.

So, keep it longer, and let the tree of investment grow. The investment tree will stop growing if you cut it down by selling it. Give it time to grow and fruit profits for you.

The Golden Rule: Don't Sell Unless Necessary

A golden rule should be: don't sell unless you have to.

By this I mean sell if you have serious financial difficulty meeting the repayment loan payments. Or selling may be appropriate after you finish working and in your retirement.

Rather than be tempted when noticing the market value seems high, and/or thinking it would be nice to reduce loan debt.

It's easy to be swayed by media commentary about "market peaks." But history shows that Australian property markets often set new records after temporary plateaus. Selling too early might leave you priced out of future growth cycles. Often, large price escalation spurts occur after long periods of plateaus, which is another reason to be patient in not selling unless you really have to.

Let the Investment Tree Grow: Long-Term Wealth Creation

I just mentioned that you want to hold the property

investment long enough to recoup the buying and selling costs.

Additionally, I often say to leave the tree planted on the property as long as possible and let it keep growing. Don't chop the tree down too early; let it grow and see where it gets to.

In fact, many property experts and property owners I have met will admit that their biggest regret is selling property too early. If you keep it longer, you don't have to worry about how much you would have made if you kept it longer. Avoid the remorse over selling it too early.

If you have a long-term strategy to hold property, it means it's always a good time to buy, as historically most properties in Australia grow in capital value. No one can guarantee this will always happen, of course, but you can look back in the Australian property market, and it will show there has been no sustained dip in the upward trend ever.

Holding properties for a long-term strategy is also a great way to defer capital gains tax in Australia. Until you sell, there is no capital gains tax. There might be some exceptions, such as in your Self-Managed Super Fund (SMSF), which taxes on some capital value appreciation on regular revaluations of property. However, Self-Managed Super Fund (SMSF) property owners in that case have other advantages, such as owning in a low-tax environment.

Holding on to properties can ignite further property purchase increases as you may have net worth increases, which might contribute to you funding further property purchases or repaying debt on property, such as your home loan.

It's best to buy your property and let time work for you, as you have seen in our property statistics we showed you earlier.

Buy First, Reflect Later

I often say buy a property and then think about it, rather than think about it and then buy a property. This is because the market is escalating, and the quicker you move into buying property, the easier it is to access a property at an affordable level, as this is escalating, and the quicker you start to make capital value and wealth growth through the property.

Buy the property, then you have the tree growing, and you can then think about it, it is then making you money.

Of course, this doesn't mean buying recklessly. It means acting decisively once your due diligence is complete, instead of over-analysing and missing the opportunity. In a rising market like Adelaide's in 2025, hesitation can cost thousands in just a few months.

Buying property, at the moment, is like a helium balloon; it is ever rising and quickly getting out of reach. So, jump up and catch it and hang on to its rise. Delay, and you may not be able to afford it again. Instead of jumping into a property purchase, now requires some courage, but it may lead you to see attractive property gains, which is a potent use of your time and creates wealth much faster than savings from your employment or business self-employment.

SHOULD YOU SELL AN INVESTMENT PROPERTY TO PAY OFF A HOME LOAN?

Why Some Consider This Option

I am often asked if it's a great idea to sell a property so that they can take the proceeds and reduce their home loan. But I'm of the opinion that this is not always a good idea.

Why Holding Property Is Often the Better Choice

I would suggest no, you should not sell that property unless you are struggling to repay the loan or afford the property.

Keep all the properties you can to let them gain capital appreciation, and that will increase your net worth and pay off all your debt faster. In fact, it's much more important to increase net worth rather than reduce debt.

So why would you repay debt and stop two properties or more from continuing to grow in value?

I know I like to talk about growing the trees of investment. Let as many property investment trees grow as you can. Chopping one down to repay loans stunts you down to today's level of capital appreciation. You may also have to pay some capital gains tax and not keep it all. We explain that later, too.

I see it as the hardest bit has been done, you got the property. Or if it was easy, you might need to appreciate it more, as in recent times it's become much more difficult to own a property. Chances are that it is harder to get a property now, so keep it longer.

You may think, ok, it's great to sell at this price now. But maybe you can't buy again after you do this sale. So, if you have the property already, just keep it longer.

Why don't you see how the high demand for properties, housing shortage demand and lack of supply go? And where your property value can go.

I am of the opinion that it just simply is not worth selling properties for capital gains of less than as a general rule of thumb $300,000. Less than that, is not enough change to pay home loans and I believe waiting longer will likely give you a better and more worthwhile gain. So, ask yourself if the capital gain is minor, think about keeping it growing longer.

Avoiding the Biggest Regret: Selling Too Soon

If you sell, you would never know what you could sell it for further down the track, would you? Well, maybe you will know and regret it. So, keep your properties as long as you can and see where the investment tree can grow to. *Remember what I said, what is most property owners' biggest remorse? Yes, selling too early and seeing what the property value of their sold property climbs to down the track.*

A great example of this is perhaps in family separations, where selling a family home around covid time and then not buying again until recently. Selling at that time, followed by the price escalation in that time since, meant it was difficult to buy again with the amount they got for the sale of the house. Let's say selling for $500,000 in 2021, meant that trying to buy another equivalent house 4 years later is around $300,000 more, as the median house price has risen so far.

Meaning it becomes unaffordable to them. This is compounded in the case of a separating couple that reduces loan affordability from a couple to a single.

I often hear lots of jokes about the property owners of various ethnic backgrounds in Australia who never sell property. Is that true? Well, I don't really know, of course, everyone is different in their financial affairs. But do I think it's a good idea? Absolutely yes. Keep your properties until at least your retirement.

Retirement is a time when income is lowered, and hence it is a more effective time to consider capital gains and realising a sale of a property. And of course, it's a great time to enjoy your wealth creation.

The lesson from 2025 remains clear: patience pays in property. Those who held onto investments during past downturns (like 2008 or 2020) often ended up with far stronger financial positions than those who sold under pressure.

Of course, I often say it is inevitable that loans will eventually be paid off with some hard work. So, picture yourself down the track, maybe when you are retired, and this property is paid off and owned outright. It will always be nice to get the rent per week as passive income.

There are other benefits too. It may be an option to use it as a home downsize option, weekend house, or retirement place. Or more importantly can be used for intergenerational wealth transfer, which is a fancy way to say an option for your kids or family to own, enjoy, or even live in it. This is becoming of greater concern, particularly to younger parents who worry about how their children are ever going to own a home in these escalating property market times.

HOMEOWNERSHIP VS. INVESTMENT PROPERTY: WHICH IS BETTER?

Why Not Strive for Both?

There's no doubt that owning your own home and investment properties are both beneficial in many ways. If you set your goals to do both, I don't see any reason why you can't own your home and investment properties. With the right planning, you can structure your finances to achieve both over time. For example, some investors choose to purchase their first property as an investment, then use the equity growth from that property to fund their own home purchase. Which one you do first is up to you and depends on your circumstances. It's crucial to seek both education and professional advice to design the right strategy for your goals...

Comparing the Benefits

The answer depends a lot on your personal situation. But let me explain some of the tax benefits of both.

First, let's look at an investment property. *I like to explain to people that the tenant is paying for most of it.* So, you buy the property, find someone to rent it to, called the tenant, and they pay you rent for living in the property.

In this situation of having an investment property which generates income, the Australian tax system allows you to claim expenses in holding the property and being made available for rent. These include interest on your loan, depreciation on the building, property rates and taxes, insurances, repairs, and maintenance.

In contrast, home ownership does not generate tax deductions, but it gives you lifestyle stability and access to the Capital Gains Tax exemption when you sell your main residence, which can be an enormous financial benefit. Owning a home is still a great property investment, and your home can still make huge capital gains and best of all, these are under the main residence exemption to capital gains tax.

Tax Deductions Available for Investment Properties

In Australia, you can claim a variety of tax deductions for rental properties. Here are some of the key deductions:

1. Advertising for tenants: Costs for advertising your rental property.

2. Body corporate fees and charges: Fees for the administration and maintenance of the property.

3. Council rates: Local government rates for the property.

4. Water charges: Costs for water usage.

5. Land tax: State government tax on the land value.

6. Interest on loans: Interest expenses on loans used to purchase the property.

7. Insurance: Premiums for building, contents, and public liability insurance.

8. Repairs and maintenance: Costs for repairs and maintenance to keep the property in good condition.

9. Cleaning: Expenses for cleaning the property.

10. Pest control: Costs for pest control services.

11. Property agent fees and commissions: Fees paid to property managers or agents.

12. Legal expenses: Costs for legal services related to the property.

13. Depreciation: Decline in the value of depreciating assets like appliances and furniture. It is important for you to consider obtaining a depreciation report prepared by suitably qualified quantity surveyors on your property less than 40 years old, to maximise your depreciation claims from when you have purchased your property for current and future tax return advantages. You can order a depreciation report here https://bit.ly/4oNQ5Nb

14. Capital works deductions: Deductions for construction costs over several years.

It's important to keep accurate records and ensure that the expenses are directly related to the rental property for 5 years or more for receipts relating to depreciation.

Understanding Negative Gearing and Its Tax Advantages

When you own an investment property, you are reporting in your tax return the net rental income of the property, which is the rent minus the expenses that were just mentioned. At times this may be a profit, but often it may be a loss. When it is a loss, it is sometimes referred to as negative gearing, this loss can be offset against other taxable income in Australia and hence may contribute to a tax refund. Typically, a rental with a high loan and high depreciation will be a rental loss, also known as negative gearing.

Despite some political debate in recent years, as of 2025 negative gearing remains available in Australia and continues to be one of the most powerful tools for property investors. This is undoubtedly one of the main reasons why buying investment property is so. Many Australians getting unsatisfying tax return refunds should consider investment in property for this reason. I have seen it take many taxpayers from minor tax deductions to major tax deductions in addition to the capital gains. This is common to these types of employees who typically have minor deductions coupled with good income for good potential investment property borrowing. These include: government workers, fly in fly out workers, professionals or even tradespersons. But even if you have deductions, more with an investment property would be beneficial to all taxpayers.

A rental loss can improve your tax position by providing an additional deduction, which may result in a larger tax refund. Since your tenant covers most of your loan costs, owning a rental property can be more affordable than having a home loan. With a home loan, you bear all the expenses yourself including the major one of interest and loan repayments, and since there is no rental income, those costs are not tax-deductible.

The extra tax refund from a net rental loss depends on your income levels called Taxable income by the Australian Tax Office.

Here are the tax rates paid by residents of Australia for tax purposes.

RESIDENT TAX RATES 2025–26

Taxable income	Tax on this income
0 – $18,200	Nil
$18,201 – $45,000	16c for each $1 over $18,200
$45,001 – $135,000	$4,288 plus 30c for each $1 over $45,000
$135,001 – $190,000	$31,288 plus 37c for each $1 over $135,000
$190,001 and over	$51,638 plus 45c for each $1 over $190,000

The above rates **do not** include the Medicare levy of 2%.

These are available in more detail on this link, https://www.ato.gov.au/tax-rates-and-codes/tax-rates-australian-residents.

Generally, whatever your tax rate is, this tax rate table, is an indicator of the amount of additional tax refund you got. For example, a net rental loss of $15000 when earning between $45000 to $135000, increases your refund by $4500 - $15000 * 30% (ignoring Medicare levy or 32% including Medicare levy an additional tax to income tax applicable to most Australians which funds our public health system).

Let's not forget this is how to calculate the approximate tax benefit per year, but the good news is that if you expand this to the remaining working career you have while you own the investment property, the tax benefits can add up to many (perhaps hundreds of) thousands of dollars. I would suggest you wait for the first full year you own your investment property and ask your accountant or do it yourself, assess the approximate tax refund increment from your investment property then times it by your remaining years until you plan to retire realistically, to know just how much tax benefits you might receive. Of course, this is a quick estimate only an actual calculation would entail assessment from every future actual tax return figure, which I do not recommend as necessary. Just sit back and enjoy your bigger refunds and keep an occasional eye on your capital gains.

The Tax-Free Advantage of Homeownership

When you own and live in a home as your primary residence, you may be eligible for a main residence exemption from capital gains tax (CGT). This means that if your home's value increases over time and you decide to sell it, you typically won't have to pay tax on the profit you make from the sale. This exemption can provide a significant financial advantage, as CGT is usually payable on the sale of investment properties or other assets.

Your home also gives lifestyle stability and long-term wealth potential. Even though homeownership doesn't offer annual tax deductions, the CGT exemption often makes it a powerful wealth strategy in its own right.

A STRATEGY FOR YOUNG BUYERS FACING AFFORDABILITY CHALLENGES

For young individuals who find it challenging to afford a home, a strategic approach could be to purchase an investment property first rather than a home to live in.

There are important factors to consider, such as first-homeowner grants and stamp duty concessions, which may help reduce upfront costs. While finding a suitable property may still be difficult, owning an investment property can offer advantages like better cash flow, since the tenant covers most of the expenses, and tax benefits associated with investment properties.

As previously mentioned, buying an investment property allows time to work in your favour, helping you build wealth through property appreciation. Over time, as your equity in the investment property grows, you may then be in a stronger financial position to purchase your own home.

If you have a partner or later enter a relationship, you could consider buying both a home and an investment property together, or simply choose to purchase a home when your financial situation allows.

This approach can make homeownership more achievable while leveraging the benefits of property investment.

I have also seen Australians consider cheaper property markets such as Victoria currently in Australia or even outside of Australia altogether. Or even instead of homes look at apartments which cost less.

Also, consider quick income spikes by working in higher income avenues from fly in fly out industries, overseas countries or just having a second hustle to gain more income. These are great ideas. I do suggest always getting tax advice on working overseas. Book in for working overseas advice with me here.

ACT QUICKLY BEFORE PRICES RISE BEYOND REACH

So again, what are you waiting for? Get in there and get that investment property.

Think of buying a property as a helium balloon rising fast, jump up and grab it, before it gets out of reach and then hang onto rise. See where the property can appreciate to, enjoy the net wealth creation, and enjoy the tax benefits, including big tax refunds along the way, get the tenant to pay for most of it, and use other people's money like your banks. Of course, you, like many others, have and continue to do this. As a tax agent, this is a tried and tested simple tax strategy that works especially in the recent property escalating environment. In practice, to do well in Australia financially it is predominantly all about buying property. Greatest wealth accumulation occurs not from employment or business income but from consistent investing. Of course, as we are explaining there are many reasons to choose property investment to speed up your net wealth creation.

BUILDING WEALTH AND PASSIVE INCOME THROUGH PROPERTY

In practice, it is one of the best ways to create wealth in Australia that is well complemented by the Australian taxation system.

The return on your time of a well-planned and sought-after investment property is fantastic compared to the bread and butter of wages and business active incomes.

Think ahead, too, you may own properties without debt one day. Imagine getting income from fully paid properties. Money for no more work, all you need to do is offer a property asset you have worked hard to own for rent.

By 2025, rents in many capital cities will have surged more than 30% in three years, which means rental yields are at their strongest levels in over a decade, making passive income from property ownership more attractive than ever.

SHOULD YOU WAIT FOR A BIGGER DEPOSIT OR PAY LENDERS MORTGAGE INSURANCE?

Why Banks Prefer a 20% Deposit

Most banks will prefer a 20% deposit towards a residential property. This may be in the form of a cash deposit, such as money in the bank put towards the residential property purchase. Alternatively, you may have equity in another property. It is typical to see that you are committed to the property purchase and have established a good savings record for the property investment. Your commitment to savings toward the property has become a common practice for lenders. You might also say the lenders want to see you go first in putting into the property as well.

To illustrate equity, form another property:

If you own a property that is valued at $600,000, the bank will value this conservatively and allocate 80% of this value as acceptable to the loan balance.

80% of $600,000 is $480,000.

Therefore, if your loan is $300,000, then you have additional equity in this house as a security property of $180,000.

So, this amount in this case $180,000, can be put towards another residential property purchase.

What Happens If You Don't Have Enough Loan Deposit?

If you lack a full deposit, banks may still approve the loan by applying **Lenders Mortgage Insurance (LMI)**. LMI usually ranges from $5,000 to $20,000.

While it feels like an extra cost, property prices continue to rise, and waiting longer may delay your entry into the market. In many cases, future capital gains will far exceed the upfront LMI cost, especially for buyers with long-term plans.

Why Paying Lenders Mortgage Insurance Can Be Worth It

If a bank approves you with LMI, it may be better to proceed instead of waiting years to save more. Delaying can push property further out of reach.

Think ahead 10–20 years. In most markets, long-term growth far outweighs the one-off LMI fee. Getting started is often the hardest step, and LMI allows you to enter the market sooner.

Newly Announced Australian Government 5% Deposit Scheme (Commencing October 2025)

From October 2025, First-Home Buyers may purchase with:

- **5% deposit**, or
- **2% deposit for single parents/legal guardians**

Key features:

- No LMI
- Unlimited places
- Must live in the home
- Price caps apply
- Government-backed approval to support lenders

This scheme reduces upfront barriers and makes homeownership more achievable.

More details: <u>https://firsthomebuyers.gov.au/australian-government-5-percent-deposit-scheme</u>

THE BENEFIT OF FORCED SAVING THROUGH HOME OWNERSHIP

Building Equity

A portion of each repayment goes toward the principal, building equity. Over time, this becomes a meaningful form of savings.

Property Appreciation

Australian property has shown strong long-term growth. Between 2015–2025, median prices in several cities more than doubled, showing how capital growth boosts net wealth.

Financial Discipline

Mortgage repayments enforce structured saving. Without such commitments, many households find it easier to spend rather than save.

Leveraging Your Equity

Equity can be used for renovations, investments, business opportunities, or purchasing additional properties. Many people sit on "lazy equity"—low loans on high-value homes—and could accelerate wealth by investing again.

Stability and Security

Owning a home protects you from rent increases and provides a long-term asset for family stability and generational wealth.

Forced saving is one of the key reasons homeownership strengthen financial stability over time.

USING TIME TO LEVERAGE YOUR PROPERTY INVESTMENT

Leveraging time is crucial in property investment for several reasons:

Compounding Growth

Property values generally appreciate over time. By holding onto a property for a longer period, you can benefit from the compounding growth of its value. This means the longer you hold the property, the more potential there is for significant appreciation.

Mortgage Amortization

As you make regular mortgage payments over time, you gradually pay down the principal loan amount. This process, known as amortization, increases your equity in the property. Over time, a larger portion of your payments goes towards the principal rather than interest, accelerating your equity growth. With interest rates easing in early 2025 after peak hikes in 2023–2024, amortization benefits have become even more noticeable for borrowers who refinanced at lower rates. Working harder to increase loan repayments gets your loan paid faster, which of course can save you thousands of dollars.

Rental Income Growth

If you rent out your property, the rental income can cover your mortgage payments and other expenses. Over time, as rents typically increase, your rental income can provide a steady and growing cash flow, enhancing your investment returns. In fact, Adelaide's rental market recorded annual growth of more than 10% in 2024–2025 due to a supply shortage, pushing gross rental yields above 4.2%. Rental property cashflow will improve over time as loan repayments reduce interest charges, along with increased rents due to increases. Better still you may even repay the loan completely.

Tax Benefits Over Time

Owning property can offer various tax benefits, such as deductions for mortgage interest, property taxes, and depreciation. These benefits can accumulate over time, reducing your overall tax burden and increasing your tax return refunds. Investors are also making use of negative gearing benefits, which remain available despite ongoing government reviews.

Riding Market Cycles

Real estate markets go through cycles of growth and correction. By holding a property over a longer period, you can ride out short-term market fluctuations and benefit from long-term trends. This reduces the risk of having to sell during a downturn. For example, while prices dipped slightly during the 2022 interest rate hikes, owners who held through to 2025 have already recovered those values and achieved fresh record highs.

Power of Leverage

Using borrowed money to finance a property allows you to control a larger asset with a smaller initial investment. Over time, as the property's value increases, the return on your initial investment can be significantly amplified. Fantastically, you can use other people's money to generate wealth. This is why leverage is considered one of the most powerful wealth-building tools available to property investors, particularly in periods of low interest rates like those beginning to re-emerge in 2025.

Property as an Inflation Hedge

Real estate often acts as a hedge against inflation. As the cost of living rises, property values and rental incomes tend to increase as well, preserving your purchasing power over time. Even during Australia's inflation spike in 2022–2023, investors benefited as rents surged while mortgage repayments remained fixed under earlier low-rate loans.

By leveraging time, property investors can maximize their returns, build substantial equity, and benefit from the various financial advantages that come with long-term property ownership. Simply put, patience in property almost always pays.

CAPITAL GAINS TAX (CGT) IN AUSTRALIA: WHAT IS IT AND HOW TO MANAGE IT?

Capital Gains Tax (CGT) in Australia is a tax on the profit you make from selling certain types of assets, such as property, shares, or businesses. Here are the key points:

How CGT Works

1. **Capital Gain or Loss**: When you sell an asset for more than you paid for it, the difference is your capital gain. If you sell it for less, you incur a capital loss.

2. **Net Capital Gains**: You pay tax on your net capital gains, which is your total capital gains minus any capital losses and any discounts you're eligible for.

3. **CGT Discount**: Australian residents who hold an asset for at least 12 months before selling it can reduce their capital gain by 50%. This means you only pay tax on half of the gain.

4. **Tax Rate:** The net capital gain is added to your taxable income and taxed at your marginal tax rate.. Taxes on your taxable income rates have been tabled earlier.

Exemptions and Special Cases

5. **Primary Residence:** Your main home is generally exempt from CGT.

6. **Inherited Assets**: Special rules apply to assets you inherit.

7. **Small Business Concessions**: There are additional concessions for small business owners.

Example CGT Calculation

If you bought an investment property for $500,000 and sold it five years later for $600,000, your capital gain would be $100,000. As you have owned the asset for more than 1 year and If you qualify for the 50% discount, you would only pay tax on $50,000. This then added to the owner's taxable income and was taxed at their marginal tax rates. If your taxable income was $100,000 before the sale, your new taxable income would be $150,000. Taxes on your taxable income rates have been tabled earlier.

Forecasting Your CGT Position Before Selling

Understanding CGT can help you make informed decisions about your investments. I would always recommend getting capital gains tax advice before selling properties. That way, you know the tax and can be happy with your selling price, with less capital gains tax. As opposed to the selling price, less an uncertain or unexpected amount of taxes down the track. With additional tax planning you can do everything you can to legally minimise your capital gains tax.

Book in for your property tax advice session at https://bit.ly/4oNQ5Nb. More information at Property Accountant Adelaide | Tax Accounting Adelaide or Expert tax Adelaide | Tax Accounting Adelaide.

There can be nothing worse than selling with the unexpected capital gains tax down the track, which may have changed your view of the selling price and position at the sale. When you have an accurate estimate of likely future capital gain taxes you are in a better position to make a more informed selling decision.

The Easiest Way to Avoid CGT Is—Don't Sell

I believe that capital gains tax is a great tax because it isn't paid unless you sell a property. You can always choose to sell the property when it suits you best for tax purposes.

Simply put, if you don't sell yet, there is no capital gains tax.

If you do plan on selling, it's a great idea to work it into your retirement when your income is usually lower or, in some cases, income tax-free, such as retirement superannuation pension payments.

Perhaps you could take a break, a year off, and have a low taxable income. Yes, some people do that. Taking a career break for travel might mean you save enough tax to pay for some travelling. Another idea is to look at maximising tax-deductible superannuation contributions in a year you are likely to have a capital gain. Again, financial planning and tax agent advice are recommended in this case.

Book in for your property tax advice session at https://bit.ly/4oNQ5Nb. More information at Property Accountant Adelaide | Tax Accounting Adelaide or Expert tax Adelaide | Tax Accounting Adelaide.

CGT on Inherited Property and Estates

Another option is to leave it in your estate, and this can have capital gains tax advantages.

When you bequeath a property in Australia, the inheritor generally doesn't pay Capital Gains Tax (CGT) at the time of inheritance. However, CGT may apply when they sell the inherited property. Here are the key points to consider:

Exemptions and Conditions

Main Residence Exemption: If the property was the main residence of the deceased and not used to produce income, they might be eligible for a full exemption from CGT if they sell the property within two years of the deceased's death.

Pre-CGT Assets: If the deceased acquired the property before 20 September 1985, it is exempt from CGT. However, any significant improvements made after this date may be subject to CGT.

Partial Exemption: If the property was used to produce income or was not the main residence of the deceased, you might qualify for a partial exemption.

Selling the Inherited Property

Within Two Years: Selling the property within two years of the deceased's death can often qualify you for a full exemption from CGT, provided the property was the main residence and not used to generate income.

After Two Years: If you sell the property after two years, CGT will generally apply. The cost base for calculating CGT is usually the market value of the property at the date of the deceased's death.

So, this is great, the original cost base of the deceased owner is therefore uplifted to the market value at the time it is bequeathed to the new inheritor/owner.

Example

If you inherit a property that was the main residence of the deceased and you sell it within two years, you may not have to pay CGT. However, if you hold onto the property for longer or it is used to produce income, CGT may apply when you sell it.

This can be a great strategy, because whoever inherits property, their cost base becomes the market value of the property at the date of the deceased person's death. So, what this means is the cost base is uplifted to the market value at the time of the inheritance.

In other words, the wait until the owner dies approach, and it goes to an estate, is a tax strategy to reset the cost base up to the current market value. This is always worth considering, particularly if you are happy and can comfortably afford to hold the property and leave it in your estate. This is an alternative to selling and getting the property sale proceeds now minus the capital gain tax. Again, this is a situation I would recommend investing in some tax agent advice.

Book in for your property tax advice session at https://bit.ly/4oNQ5Nb. More information at Property Accountant Adelaide | Tax Accounting Adelaide or Expert tax Adelaide | Tax Accounting Adelaide.

Special Rules For Foreign Residents

Special rules apply if the deceased or the beneficiary is a foreign resident. Generally, foreign residents are not entitled to the main residence exemption. Since July 2023, foreign residents selling Australian property above $750,000 are also subject to a 12.5% withholding tax at settlement, which directly affects CGT outcomes.

REASONS TO BUY PROPERTY IN AUSTRALIA NOW DESPITE AFFORDABILITY CHALLENGES

Buying property in Australia now, despite affordability challenges, can still be a wise decision for several reasons:

Long-Term Investment Potential

- **Capital Growth**: Historically, Australian property values have appreciated over time. Investing now can allow you to benefit from long-term capital growth.

- **Stable Market:** Australia's property market is considered stable and resilient, making it a reliable investment even during economic fluctuations.

- **Current Data:** As of 2025, CoreLogic reports that the national median dwelling price has risen by more than 35% since 2020, proving that even buyers who purchased during perceived "peaks" have still gained substantial equity.

Tax Advantages

- **Negative Gearing:** Investors can offset property losses against their taxable income, reducing their overall tax burden.

- **Capital Gains Tax Exemptions:** If the property is your main residence, you may be exempt from paying capital gains tax when you sell it.

- **Depreciation Deductions:** Investors can also claim depreciation on fixtures, fittings, and building structure, further lowering taxable income. This remains a major advantage in 2025 for newly built or recently renovated properties. Here is how to order a depreciation report. If you own an investment property, you need one of our reports; otherwise you are potentially missing out on thousands of dollar's worth of tax deductions. Here https://bit.ly/4oNQ5Nb.

Depreciation is a way of following the tax rules, whereby major asset expenditure cannot be claimed immediately. But rather systematically over the years of the useful life of the assets. Claiming depreciation is the right and legal way to avoid tax audit risk and lead to significant tax savings and improved cash flow.

Low-Interest Rates

- **Current Rates:** While interest rates have risen from historic lows, they are still relatively low compared to past decades. Locking in a mortgage now can secure favourable terms before potential future increases.

- **Lending Flexibility:** Major banks and second-tier lenders are now offering green home loans and cash-back offers to attract borrowers, making finance slightly more competitive in 2025.

Government Incentives

- **First-Home Buyer Grants:** Various state and federal grants and concessions are available to first-time buyers, making it easier to enter the market. The government 5% deposit scheme was explained earlier.

- **Stamp Duty Concessions:** Some states offer stamp duty concessions for first-time-buyers, reducing the upfront costs of purchasing a property.

- **Shared Equity Schemes:** In 2025, federal and state governments are expanding shared equity schemes where the government co-invests with buyers, lowering the deposit hurdle.

- **The new 5% government home-buying scheme.** As previously explained.

Rental Income Opportunities

- **High Demand:** Rental demand remains strong in many areas, providing a steady income stream for investors.

- **Rental Yield:** With rising rents, the rental yield on properties can be attractive, helping to cover mortgage payments and other expenses.

- **Current Market:** In 2025, vacancy rates in capital cities remain below 1.2%, and rents have climbed more than 9% annually, ensuring solid returns for landlords.

Personal and Lifestyle Benefits

- **Stability:** Owning a home provides stability and security, allowing you to settle in a community and avoid the uncertainties of renting.

- **Customization:** Homeownership gives you the freedom to renovate and personalize your living space to suit your preferences.

- **Intergenerational Wealth:** For many Australians, property remains the primary way to build and pass on wealth to children, making ownership a cornerstone of family security.

Future-Proofing Your Finances

- **Hedge Against Inflation:** Real estate often acts as a hedge against inflation, preserving your purchasing power over time.

- **Retirement Planning:** Owning property can be a key part of your retirement strategy, providing a valuable asset that can be sold or leveraged in the future.

- **Superannuation Strategy:** Self-Managed Superannuation Funds (SMSF) continue to allow property investment, letting Australians combine retirement savings with long-term property growth. Yes, why not consider unlocking some of your super savings to buy a property by your SMSF either outright or with a loan called limited recourse borrowing arrangements? The great thing about buying property in your super is that it is owned in a low-taxed environment, taxed at only 15% pre-retirement and no tax post-retirement. SMSF can also allow you to pool your super funds with your spouse or family. You are also able to invest in more than just financial investments like normal super funds. For instance, you can invest in direct shares, crypto, property, collectibles and precious metals such as gold. Of course, again seeking financial advice on the costs and whether a SMSF is right for you is recommended. Being active in your investment can see a greater rate of return too.

Despite the challenges, buying property now can offer significant long-term benefits. Yes, affordability is tough in 2025, but delaying may only push buyers further out of the market as values and rents continue to climb.

ROMEO'S TOP TIPS

PROPERTY VS. SHARES: WHICH IS THE BETTER INVESTMENT?

The performance of the property market versus shares in Australia can vary depending on the time frame and specific market conditions. Here's a comparison based on recent data:

Property Market Performance

Long-Term Growth: Over the past 25 years, Australian house prices have risen by an average of 6.8% per year.

Recent Performance: In FY24, the national median property price rose by 8%, and when rental income is included, the total return for property investors was around 12.2%.

Share Market Performance

Long-Term Growth: The Australian share market has generated an average return of 9.7% per year over the last 20 years.

Recent Performance: The S&P/ASX 200 Index rose by 7.83% in FY24, and with dividends included, the total return was approximately 12.1%.

Key Considerations Beyond Returns

Liquidity: Shares are more liquid than property, meaning they can be bought and sold more quickly and with lower transaction costs.

Tangibility: Property is a tangible asset that you can physically manage and improve, while shares represent ownership in a company.

- **Tax Efficiency**: Both asset classes offer tax benefits. Property investors can benefit from negative gearing and depreciation, while share investors can benefit from franking credits on dividends.

- **Entry Costs:** Investing in shares typically has lower entry costs compared to property, which involves significant upfront expenses like stamp duty and legal fees.

Conclusion

Both property and shares have their own advantages and risks. Historically, shares have offered higher average returns, but property provides the stability of a tangible asset and potential for rental income. The best choice depends on your personal financial goals, risk tolerance, and investment horizon.

In practice, it's important that you find the weapon of investment that suits you and that you like the best. It's a bit like choosing your favourite colour or car. It is entirely up to you, and I think both shares and property are fantastic investments. I also feel like buying a property is a much simpler decision, whereas there are more variety and knowledge, and any information required to be a good share investor.

I personally do both. I find share equity accumulation a great way to launch the equity and savings accumulation quickly in between buying other properties. It can be a way to gain more net wealth by getting higher returns than paying off your bank loans. By trying to your loan rate by getting a higher return on your share investments. This can be easier with shares as you can invest with smaller amounts. As against property investments which may need bigger amounts to accumulate before you are ready to shoot the arrow and buy another property. So, I think share investment can be a great interim investment while waiting to buy a property.

It is certainly much more tax-effective if shares have Australian franking credits, which means the dividend income has some tax already paid. Franked dividends are much more tax effective than bank interest earned another classic interim investment while waiting to buy a property. Not only is your interest income yield quite low in present times, but it is also fully taxed at your marginal tax rates, which in some cases is at least 30%. This makes earning bank interest very tax inefficient.

In my experience as an accountant, I have also seen many clients buy shares and develop fantastic share portfolios as late as their forties and fifties and develop wonderful wealth in share portfolios.

In 2025, many Australians are building hybrid portfolios—using property as the foundation of long-term stability, while adding shares for liquidity and higher compounding growth.

Rather than just reducing debt, keep investing.

I also believe that rather than just aiming to reduce debt on a home or investment property, investing in shares that outperform your loan interest rate is an excellent way.

Put another way, rather than putting all your spare change into reducing debt, invest more. Get investment advisers or if you are confident, invest alone. With the aim of outswimming your home loan interest costs. This will help you repay your debt even faster and create greater wealth.

WHY RESIDENTIAL PROPERTY IN AUSTRALIA IS CONSIDERED LOW-RISK?

Residential property in Australia is often considered a low-risk investment for several reasons:

Historical Stability

- **Long-Term Growth**: Historically, Australian property values have shown consistent long-term growth. <u>Even during economic downturns, the property market has demonstrated resilience and a tendency to recover.</u>

- **Low Volatility:** Compared to other investment options like stocks, the property market tends to be less volatile, providing a more stable investment environment.

Strong and Sustained Demand

- **Population Growth**: Australia's population continues to grow, driven by both natural increase and immigration. <u>This sustained demand for housing supports property values.</u>

- **Urbanization:** Increasing urbanization and the concentration of population in major cities like Sydney, Melbourne, and Brisbane drive demand for residential properties.

Government Support and Regulation

- **Incentives and Grants:** The Australian government

offers various incentives and grants for homebuyers, such as the First Home Owner Grant and stamp duty concessions, which support the property market.

- **Regulatory Framework**: A robust regulatory framework ensures transparency and stability in the property market, protecting both buyers and investors.

Favourable Economic Conditions

- **Low Interest Rates**: Historically low interest rates have made borrowing more affordable, encouraging property investment.

- **Strong Economy**: Australia's relatively strong and stable economy supports the property market by maintaining employment levels and consumer confidence.

Rental Market Strength

- **High Rental Demand:** With a growing population and limited housing supply, rental demand remains strong, providing a steady income stream for property investors.

- **Low Vacancy Rates:** Low vacancy rates in many areas ensure that rental properties are occupied, reducing the risk of prolonged vacancies.

Portfolio Diversification

- **Asset Diversification**: Property investment provides diversification in an investment portfolio, reducing overall risk by spreading investments across different asset classes.

Protection Against Inflation

- **Protection Against Inflation:** Real estate often acts as a hedge against inflation, as property values and rental incomes tend to rise with inflation, preserving the purchasing power of your investment.

These factors contribute to the perception of residential property in Australia as a low-risk investment.

WHY CONTINUE WORKING EVEN IF YOU OWN MULTIPLE PROPERTIES?

Multiple property owners in Australia often continue to work for several reasons, and negative gearing is indeed a significant factor. Here's a detailed look:

The Role of Negative Gearing

Negative gearing allows property investors to deduct the losses they incur from their rental properties against their other income, such as salary or wages. This can significantly reduce their taxable income, making property investment more attractive. However, to benefit from negative gearing, investors need to have other income to offset these losses, which is one reason they continue to work.

In other words, without other salary income, the rental loss deduction would be wasted. In 2025, negative gearing remains untouched despite political debate, but many investors fear potential reform, making salaried income even more valuable for tax efficiency.

Financial Security and Stability

Having a regular job provides a stable and predictable source of income, which is essential for managing personal and family expenses. <u>This stability is particularly important given the potential fluctuations in rental income due to vacancies or market conditions</u>. Working income also helps investors meet stricter lending requirements imposed by banks in 2025, which often require stable PAYG income to approve additional loans.

Reinvestment and Portfolio Growth

Many property owners use their job income to reinvest in their properties or to purchase additional properties. This strategy helps them grow their real estate portfolio more quickly and take advantage of new investment opportunities.

Risk Management

Relying solely on rental income can be risky due to market fluctuations, maintenance costs, and potential vacancies. Having a job provides a safety net and reduces financial risk, ensuring they can cover their expenses even during challenging times.

Lifestyle and Personal Fulfillment

For some, their job is a source of personal fulfillment and professional growth. They may enjoy their work and find it rewarding beyond the financial benefits. Continuing to work allows them to pursue their passions and maintain a sense of purpose. I often say, it is great to continue to win at something and work can provide a sense of achievement. Some may feel they are still getting back at work and desire more success in this area of their life. Many may say they aren't ready to stop working, they may get bored without it and that time off is enough for their leisure.

Social and Professional Networks

Working in a job helps maintain and expand social and professional networks. These connections can be valuable for personal growth, career advancement, and even finding new investment opportunities.

Tax Efficiency Advantages

Negative gearing, combined with the capital gains tax discount, makes property investment particularly tax-efficient. This combination allows investors to offset rental losses against their taxable income and benefit from reduced tax on capital gains when they sell the property.

Overall, while negative gearing is a significant factor, multiple property owners continue to work for a combination of financial security, growth opportunities, risk management, and personal fulfillment.

It is great to retire with passive income. Owing property outright at retirement is ideal. There is nothing better than receiving passive rental income when you retire. After all, you have deserved it and it is time to enjoy your retirement living affordably and happily with financial freedom.

Better still, if you have paid it off before you retire, the passive income is even greater. In 2025, with rental yields so high and superannuation rules becoming stricter, many investors see property income as their true retirement safety net.

Why have the uncertain future and try to rely on the Australian pension to support your retirement when you can invest in superannuation and other investments like property to make our financial freedom pre-and post-retirement.

WHY INCOME PROTECTION IS ESSENTIAL WHEN NEGATIVE GEARING IN AUSTRALIA?

Protecting your income-by-income protection insurance is crucial if you are negative gearing in Australia for several reasons:

Covering Shortfalls

Negative gearing means your rental income is less than your property expenses, resulting in a loss. This loss is offset against your other income, such as your salary. If your primary income source is disrupted, you may struggle to cover these shortfalls, leading to financial stress. In other words, the negative gearing deductions would be lost in the unfortunate circumstances of injury or sickness stopping your income. But with income protection insurances that pay you income in these circumstances of sickness and injury, your continued income can continue to gain tax benefits and tax refunds from the negative gearing deductions.

Maintaining Cash Flow

A steady income ensures you can meet ongoing property expenses like mortgage repayments, maintenance, and insurance. Without sufficient income, you might face difficulties in maintaining your property, which could affect its value and rental appeal. With current mortgage rates (2025) still higher than the long-term average, maintaining cash flow is more critical than ever. Income protection provides a monthly benefit to keep your investment afloat.

Preserving Tax Benefits

Negative gearing relies on having taxable income to offset your property losses. <u>If your income drops significantly, you won't be able to fully utilize the tax benefits of negative gearing, reducing its overall financial advantage</u>. Maintaining income will utilise the rental loss deductions.

Income protection insurance. Like tax agent fees are generally tax-deductible too.

Ensuring Financial Stability

Having a secure income provides a safety net, allowing you to manage unexpected expenses or periods of vacancy without compromising your financial stability. <u>This is especially important in a fluctuating rental market</u>.

Supporting Investment Growth

A stable income allows you to reinvest in your property or expand your portfolio. <u>This can include making improvements to increase rental yield or purchasing additional properties to diversify your investments</u>. Lenders also look for stable income when approving further loans, without it, portfolio expansion becomes impossible.

Risk Management

Income protection helps mitigate the risks associated with property investment. It ensures you can continue to meet your financial obligations even in unforeseen circumstances, such as job loss or illness.

Overall, protecting your income is essential for maintaining the benefits of negative gearing and ensuring long-term financial health.

HOW LIFE INSURANCE SUPPORTS NEGATIVELY GEARED INVESTORS IN AUSTRALIA?

Life insurance can be a crucial safety net for property investors who are negatively gearing in Australia. Here's how it can help:

Financial Security for Dependents

If you pass away, life insurance can provide a lump sum payment to your beneficiaries. This can help cover outstanding mortgage debts and other expenses, ensuring your family isn't burdened with financial stress. They may have time to manage the property asset easily with a life insurance payment and therefore have less need to sell the property in the short-term.

Covering Outstanding Debts

Life insurance can help pay off the mortgage on your negatively geared property. This ensures that your family doesn't have to sell the property under distressing circumstances or face financial hardship due to the outstanding debt.

Sustaining Investment Strategy

The payout from a life insurance policy can help maintain your investment strategy. <u>Your family can use the funds to continue managing the property, covering costs like maintenance, property management fees, and other expenses, allowing them to benefit from potential long-term capital gains.</u>

Tax Advantages of Life Insurance

While life insurance premiums are generally not tax-deductible, the benefits received from a life insurance policy are usually tax-free. This can provide a significant financial boost to your family without additional tax burdens.

Peace of Mind for Investors

Knowing that your family will be financially secure if something happens to you can provide peace of mind. This allows you to focus on your investment strategy without worrying about the potential financial impact on your loved ones.

Overall, life insurance can be an essential part of a comprehensive financial plan for property investors who are negatively gearing, providing financial security and stability for your family in the event of your death.

If you can afford life insurance and have high debt levels, it can make a difficult situation like death much easier. The estate can more easily continue to run the property portfolio as debt is paid from life insurance.

COPING WITH THE OBJECTION OF I HATE HAVING DEBT?

A common objection I hear from clients when I explain why buying a property is tax beneficial is they say but I hate having debt or something like that … I just hate having debt.

On one hand, as I explained in the question should I sell investment property to reduce debt, I said maybe not as the property will continue to appreciate and help your grow net wealth.

Similarly acquiring more property with debt will also help you improve your net worth position in time.

Besides paying off debt is inevitable; you will get there. Simply stick to your loan repayments or pay it off even quicker if you can.

Do not continually think of having debt and being in debt as that can make it feel like a life sentence of hard work.

However, owning property as explained in this book can be very financially rewarding in Australia. So, if you can buy more property, be proactive and take action.

Don't wait if you can do it now.

Don't let having more loans stop you.

Well in addition to all the wonderful reasons why owning property gives. Part of the journey to building wealth in properties includes having debt so you do need to try to get better at being at ease when having property loans.

Think of having debt as a bad thing… wrong think of having net wealth and is it growing by using other people's money. Rather than see it as important how much your debt is. Remind yourself it is more important how much your net wealth is which is property value less loan debt.

In fact, think of more debt as a great thing as a step to have more property investment to create more wealth.

So, remember, Debt will inevitably be paid off.

When debt is paid off – you are really on your way to

financial freedom.

Try instead of just repaying debt with every spare cent in loan repayment, to instead reinvest in shares or property. As you may recall, I am pro-investing that will give you a return of better than the current interest rate. Investing effectively that outswims your interest rate will see you gaining more net wealth and effectively repaying that debt even faster.

Remember that good debt for property investment bring so much tax savings because of negative gearing.

ADVANTAGES OF HOMEOWNERSHIP IN AUSTRALIA AND THE CAPITAL GAINS TAX MAIN RESIDENCE EXEMPTION

Advantages of Home Ownership in Australia

- Financial Stability and Security: Owning a home provides long-term financial stability. Unlike renting, where costs can increase, mortgage payments on a fixed-rate loan remain constant.
- Building Equity: Each mortgage payment increases your equity in the property, which can be a significant financial asset over time.
- Capital Growth Potential: Historically, property values in Australia have appreciated, offering potential for long-term capital growth.
- Forced Savings: Having loan commitments can be a good thing as it forces you to save and reduce loan debt. Without it, you would most likely spend more on unnecessary expenditure.

- Retirement Asset: A home can be a valuable asset for retirement, either through downsizing or using equity release schemes.

- Sense of Ownership: Owning a home provides a sense of pride and control over your living environment, allowing you to make modifications and improvements as you see fit.

- Community Engagement: Homeowners often feel more connected to their communities and are more likely to participate in local activities.

- Tax Benefits: Homeowners cannot benefit from tax deductions on mortgage interest and property taxes on their home. But they can sell the home without capital gains tax as this is exempt as previously mentioned.

Capital Gains Tax (CGT) Main Residence Exemption

The main residence exemption is a significant benefit for homeowners in Australia. Here's how it works:

Full Exemption: If the property is your main residence for the entire period, you own it, you are generally exempt from paying CGT when you sell it.

1. **Eligibility Conditions**:

   o The property must be your main residence.

   o It must not have been used to produce income (e.g., rented out or used for business).

   o The land must be 2 hectares or less.

2. **Partial Exemption**: If the property was your main residence for only part of the ownership period, you might be eligible for a partial exemption. <u>The CGT is calculated based on the proportion of time the property was your main residence</u>.

3. **6-Year Rule:** If you move out and rent the property, you can still treat it as your main residence for up to six years, provided you do not treat another property as your main residence during this period.

Example

If you bought a house and lived in it as your main residence for 10 years, then rented it out for 3 years before selling it, you could apply the 6-year rule to claim the main residence exemption for the entire period, avoiding CGT.

Understanding these benefits and exemptions can help you make informed decisions about homeownership and property investment in Australia.

WHY CONSIDER BUYING A NEW INVESTMENT PROPERTY IN AUSTRALIA? DEPRECIATION POTENTIAL AND NEGATIVE GEARING BENEFITS?

Buying a new investment property in Australia can be advantageous for several reasons, particularly due to depreciation potential and better negative gearing tax benefits. Here's a detailed look at why:

Depreciation Potential

1. **Higher Depreciation Deductions**: New properties offer significant depreciation benefits. You can claim depreciation on both the building structure (Division 43) and plant and equipment (Division 40). This can lead to substantial tax deductions over time.

   o **Building Structure**: You can claim 2.5% of the construction cost annually for up to 40 years.

   o **Plant and Equipment**: Items like appliances and fixtures can be depreciated at higher rates, providing more immediate tax benefits.

   2025 Update: Investors buying second-hand residential properties after May 2017 cannot claim depreciation on previously used plant and equipment. This makes new properties far more tax-efficient compared to older ones.

Negative Gearing Benefits

1. **Offsetting Losses**: Negative gearing allows you to offset the losses from your investment property against your other taxable income. This can reduce your overall tax liability, making property investment more financially viable.

2. **Tax Efficiency**: The combination of depreciation and negative gearing can significantly enhance the tax efficiency of your investment. The higher depreciation deductions from a new property can increase the amount of loss you can offset against

your income.

Additional Advantages of New Properties

1. **Tenant Appeal**: New properties are often more attractive to tenants due to modern amenities, energy efficiency, and lower maintenance requirements. This can lead to higher rental yields and lower vacancy rates.

2. **Lower Maintenance Costs**: New properties typically require less maintenance and come with builder warranties, reducing your ongoing expenses.

3. **Government Incentives**: There are often government incentives for purchasing new properties, such as grants and stamp duty concessions, which can reduce your upfront costs.

Conclusion

Investing in a new property can provide substantial financial benefits through depreciation and negative gearing, while also offering advantages in terms of tenant appeal and lower maintenance costs.

WHY INVEST IN A LARGE BLOCK OF PROPERTY IN AUSTRALIA? DEVELOPMENT POTENTIAL AND LAND APPRECIATION

Buying a big block property in Australia can be advantageous for several reasons, primarily focusing on property development potential and land value. Here's a detailed look at both aspects:

Property Development Potential

1. **Subdivision Opportunities**: Larger blocks often have the potential to be subdivided into smaller lots, allowing you to sell parts of the land or develop multiple properties. This can significantly increase your return on investment.

2. **Building Flexibility**: A bigger block provides more flexibility in terms of building options. You can construct a larger home, add additional structures like granny flats, or develop multi-unit dwellings.

3. **Future Development**: As urban areas expand, large blocks in desirable locations can become prime targets for future development projects, increasing their value. You may even want to take that on yourself. Property development requires specialised tax advice and tax planning.

   Book in for your property tax advice session at https://bit.ly/4oNQ5Nb. More information at Property Accountant Adelaide | Tax Accounting Adelaide or Expert tax Adelaide | Tax Accounting Adelaide.

   .

Land Value Advantages

1. **Scarcity**: Land is a finite resource, and larger blocks are becoming increasingly scarce, especially in urban and coastal areas. This scarcity can drive up the value of the land over time.

2. **Appreciation**: Historically, land values tend to

appreciate, particularly in high-demand areas. Owning a larger block can mean greater capital growth potential. Keep this rule of thumb in mind: Land appreciates and buildings depreciate. Hence the more land in your property portfolio the higher the potential property appreciation.

3. **Investment Security**: Land is a tangible asset that generally holds its value well, providing a secure investment compared to more volatile assets like stocks.

Additional Benefits

1. **Lifestyle**: Larger blocks offer more space for outdoor activities, gardening, and privacy, enhancing your quality of life.

2. **Environmental Impact**: Owning a larger piece of land allows for more sustainable living options, such as installing solar panels, rainwater tanks, and creating green spaces.

Conclusion

In 2025, buying a big block is as much about future-proofing as it is about lifestyle. With increasing demand for medium-density housing, big blocks in prime locations will likely be rezoned and become highly valuable development sites. Both property development potential and land value are compelling reasons to consider buying a big block property in Australia. The choice ultimately depends on your investment goals and personal preferences.

WHY BUYING PROPERTY NEAR GOOD FACILITIES MATTERS FOR CAPITAL GROWTH IN AUSTRALIA?

Buying property near good facilities is crucial for capital gain potential in Australia for several reasons:

High Demand Drivers

- **Desirability**: Properties close to amenities such as schools, shopping centers, public transport, and recreational facilities are highly desirable. This increased demand often leads to higher property values.

- **Tenant Appeal**: For rental properties, proximity to good facilities attracts quality tenants who are willing to pay higher rents, ensuring a steady rental income. In 2025, with rental demand at record highs in major cities, proximity to public transport and schools has become one of the top three tenant priorities.

Convenience and Lifestyle Appeal

- **Quality of Life**: Access to good facilities enhances the quality of life for residents. This makes properties in such locations more attractive to potential buyers and renters, driving up demand and prices.

- **Walkability**: Areas with high walkability scores, where residents can easily walk to shops, parks, and public transport, are particularly sought after. Post-COVID, lifestyle-driven demand has made walkable neighbourhoods outperform car-dependent suburbs in capital growth.

Infrastructure Development

- **Future Growth**: Properties near planned or ongoing infrastructure projects, such as new transport links or commercial developments, often see significant capital growth as these projects enhance the area's accessibility and appeal.

- **Government Investment**: Areas receiving government investment in infrastructure tend to experience increased property values due to improved facilities and services. Tracking government infrastructure budgets has become a smart strategy for investors in 2025.

Market Stability and Security

- **Lower Vacancy Rates**: Properties in well-facilitated areas tend to have lower vacancy rates, ensuring consistent rental income and reducing the risk of prolonged vacancies.

- **Resale Value**: When it comes time to sell, properties near good facilities generally sell faster and at higher prices due to their desirability. Agents in 2025 report that "location convenience" is now the #1 selling point, overtaking property size.

Economic and Employment Factors

- **Employment Opportunities**: Proximity to business districts and employment hubs increases the attractiveness of a property, as people prefer to live close to their workplaces.

- **Economic Resilience**: Areas with diverse facilities and strong infrastructure tend to be more economically resilient, maintaining property values even during economic downturns. For example, properties within 5km of CBDs saw price declines of less than half compared to outer suburbs during the 2022–23 interest rate hikes.

Investing in property near good facilities can significantly enhance your capital gain potential by ensuring high demand, better rental yields, and long-term value appreciation.

WHY BUYING PROPERTIES NEAR CITIES AND COASTAL AREAS ARE AMONG THE BEST PROPERTY INVESTMENTS IN AUSTRALIA?

Buying property near cities and coastal areas in Australia is often considered a great investment for several reasons:

High Demand: Properties in these areas are in high demand due to their desirable locations. Coastal properties offer scenic views and a relaxed lifestyle, while city properties provide easy access to amenities and employment opportunities. In 2025, "blue-chip" suburbs within 10km of capital city CBDs and coastal lifestyle regions like the Sunshine Coast, Byron Bay, and Mornington Peninsula remain the most competitive.

Strong Rental Yields: Both city and coastal properties tend to have strong rental yields. Coastal areas attract tourists and holidaymakers, while city areas attract professionals and students.

With international migration at record highs in 2025, city rental demand has surged, pushing yields up significantly.

Capital Growth: Historically, properties in these locations have shown strong capital growth. Coastal properties benefit from their limited supply and high demand, while city properties benefit from ongoing urban development and infrastructure improvements. According to 2025 CoreLogic data, inner-city units and prime coastal homes have outperformed the national average by 15% over the last 3 years.

Lifestyle Benefits: Coastal living offers a unique lifestyle with access to beaches, water sports, and a relaxed atmosphere. City living provides cultural attractions, dining, shopping, and entertainment options. Lifestyle migration trends post-pandemic continues to boost coastal regions, particularly where NBN and hybrid working options are strong.

Infrastructure and Amenities: Both city and coastal areas typically have well-developed infrastructure, including transportation, healthcare, and educational facilities, making them attractive places to live. Investors should monitor new projects like hospital expansions and university campuses, which increase long-term demand.

Resilience to Market Fluctuations: Properties in prime locations like cities and coastal areas tend to be more resilient to market fluctuations, maintaining their value better during economic downturns.

Conclusion

These factors make near-city and near-coastal properties some of the best places to buy property in Australia.

My rule of thumb in 2025 is simple: "If it's close to the city or the coast, it will almost always outperform."

DOES THE PROPERTY PASS THE "WOULD YOU LIKE LIVING IN IT YOURSELF" TEST?

Understanding the Property's Potential

Comfort and Suitability: By imagining yourself living in the property, you can better assess its comfort, layout, and suitability for daily living. This helps ensure the property meets your needs and preferences.

Identifying Hidden Issues: Living in a property, even hypothetically, can help you identify potential issues that might not be obvious during a brief inspection. This includes things like noise levels, natural light, and the overall feel of the space.

Investment Perspective

Market Appeal: If you find the property appealing, chances are others will too. This can be beneficial if you plan to rent it out or sell it in the future, as properties that are comfortable to live in tend to attract more interest.

Resale Value: Properties that are well-suited for living generally maintain or increase their value better over time. Thinking about living in the property yourself can help you choose a home that will be a good long-term investment.

Financial Considerations

Affordability: Considering whether you could live in the property helps you realistically assess the costs associated with it, including mortgage payments, maintenance, and utilities. This ensures you are financially prepared for homeownership.

Future Flexibility: If your circumstances change, such as needing to move for work or family reasons, having a property you could comfortably live in yourself provides flexibility. You can move in if needed, rather than being forced to sell or rent it out under less favourable conditions.

Emotional Connection

Personal Satisfaction: Owning a property you genuinely like and could see yourself living in can provide a sense of pride and satisfaction. This emotional connection can make the challenges of homeownership more rewarding.

Community Integration: Considering living in the property helps you evaluate the neighbourhood and community, ensuring it aligns with your lifestyle and values. This can enhance your overall quality of life.

LAND TAXES AND MINIMISING THEM

Land tax is generally applied to property. These are state taxes and therefore there are general tax rates pertaining to properties in each state. Each state's land tax thresholds can be found on their websites.

Land taxes are basically assessed on the land value of property. This may be different from the total value of the property because it does not include the building value of the property only the land value.

Land Taxes may have some exemptions for instance, common ones are your main home is typically exempt from land tax, primary production land such as family land may be exempt from land tax.

Each state obviously has different rates of levying land tax.

To find out more about each states land tax I have gather the related website links for you.

Land tax in Victoria

Land tax | State Revenue Office

Land tax in Victoria is calculated on the total value of all taxable land you own. The rates are progressive, starting from a tax-free threshold of $50,000 for general land. The rates increase to a maximum marginal rate of 2.65% as the land value increases. There are different rates that apply to trusts.

Land tax in New South Wales

Land tax | Revenue NSW

NSW applies a progressive land tax system with a tax-free threshold of $1,075,000 as of 2024. Above this, the rates start at $100 plus 1.6% of the land value above the general threshold. This increases to 2% for land valued over $6,571,000, which is known as the premium threshold.

Land tax in Queensland

Calculate your land tax

Queensland's land tax rates are tiered on the total value of your taxable land. The general threshold is $600,000, with a separate threshold for companies and trustees at $350,000. The rates range from 1% to 2.75%, with additional surcharges for absentee owners and foreign investors.

Land tax in South Australia

Land Tax | RevenueSA

South Australia has a tax-free threshold of $668,000. Above this, land tax is calculated at progressive rates starting from 0.5% and increasing up to 2.4% for land values exceeding $2,500,000.

Land tax in Western Australia

Land tax assessment

In Western Australia, the tax-free threshold is $300,000. Above this, rates range from 0.25% to 2.67%, with higher rates applied to land owned by non-residents and special trusts.

Land tax in the Australian Capital Territory (ACT) and Northern Territory

Land tax | ACT Revenue Office - Website

The ACT has progressive land tax rates based on the unimproved land value. The rates start at a fixed charge of $1,535 plus 0.54% for land values up to $150,000, increasing to a maximum of 1.14% for land values over

$2,000,000.

The Northern Territory does not impose land tax.

Some clients ask me will I have to pay a lot of land tax if I own properties or investment properties?

To answer that the answer is generally yes if you own a lot of properties in one state. To give you an idea I have the various Australia states land tax rates above.

If you are paying a lot of land tax in any state because you own a lot of properties in that state. I would suggest buying no further properties in that state and buying properties in other states where you have not used your land tax threshold.

Again, speak to an adviser on your land tax planning especially when you are acquiring new properties.

Conclusion

Overall, thinking about whether you could live in a property yourself helps ensure it meets your needs, is a sound investment, and provides financial and emotional benefits. I believe it helps to be guided by this golden rule: only buy a property if you would want to live in it yourself. Conversely, if you wouldn't want to live in it, don't expect others to, and long-term property value will be compromised.

WHAT ARE SOME OF THE RISKS OF OWNING PROPERTY

Some of the little-known risks of property investment are:

Employment Risk

Income loss or uncertainty through business downfall or employment insecurity, contributing to failure to repay loans, can threaten your property ownership goals. With casual and gig economy work rising in 2025, stable income is more critical than ever.

Relationship Breakdowns

Marriages and relationships breakdowns, which mean properties are sold within a short-term, not allowing any capital growth, resulting in losses from the property purchase and selling costs. You could seek to mitigate some of these risks from a family lawyer. Alternatively, you could consider unstable relationships whenever buying property as perhaps a time to pause.

Business Risks

Business risks that may seek personal assets can threaten property investment. So, let's say a plumber is negligent, causing $1m lawsuit to be pursued against him. This may expose his individual wealth in properties. Asset protection strategies need to be in place to mitigate these risks, such as trading as a company, which keeps wealth assets outside of it trading entity. Some other strategies lawyers use is to create charges to individually owned properties that rank above legal suits.

Trading entities should not own property assets. As a general rule it is best to keep trading entities separate from investment that own property. So that in case of legal suit or business failure the property assets are held outside of the business entity, protecting them from legal claims.

Inadequate Personal Insurances

Not having adequate personal insurance such as income protection insurance or life insurance. It is vital that you have some income protection to maintain the value of your property tax deductions. You see, property deductions are valueless if your income reduces to less than the tax-free threshold. This can be prevented or mitigated by having income protection insurance if sickness or accidents occur. A good financial planner can assist you with these.

Over-Borrowing

I believe and recommend only having one or two negatively geared properties to improve your tax deductions. More than that is potentially financially stressful. After owning 1 or 2 negatively geared properties, try to create wealth in a low tax environment such as superannuation, and pay off the loans to own properties outright at or before retirement.

Market Risk

Property values can fluctuate due to economic conditions, interest rates, and supply-demand dynamics. In some circumstances market conditions may mean your chosen property has reduced its value to less than purchase value. This risk may be reduced by keeping the property for the long-term.

Liquidity Risk:

Real estate is not a liquid asset, meaning it can take time to sell a property if needed.

Interest Rate Risk

Rising interest rates can increase mortgage repayments, affecting affordability and investment returns.

Tenant Risk

Difficult or destructive tenants can cause financial strain through unpaid rent or property damage. A good real estate agent can manage your property and reduce this risk. Some of the values of having a good agent are

Benefits of Using a Rental Agent

Having a rental agent in Australia can offer several advantages, especially for property owners looking to maximize their investment while minimizing stress. Here are some key benefits:

- Expert Market Knowledge – Rental agents understand local property trends, rental rates, and demand, helping landlords set competitive prices.
- Tenant Screening – They vet potential tenants thoroughly, checking references, rental history, and financial stability to reduce the risk of problematic renters.
- Legal Compliance – Rental laws and regulations can be complex. Agents ensure landlords comply with tenancy laws, lease agreements, and eviction procedures.
- Property Maintenance & Repairs – Agents coordinate maintenance and repairs, ensuring the property remains in good condition while handling tenant requests.

- Rent Collection & Financial Management – They manage rent payments, late fees, and financial records, making it easier for landlords to track income and expenses.
- Minimized Vacancy Periods – With access to a broad network of potential tenants, agents can quickly fill vacancies and reduce downtime.
- Handling Disputes – If issues arise, such as late payments or property damage, agents mediate disputes and take necessary legal action.
- Time & Stress Savings – Managing a rental property can be time-consuming. A rental agent takes care of the day-to-day responsibilities, allowing landlords to focus on other priorities.

Overall, hiring a rental agent can make property management more efficient and profitable while ensuring compliance with regulations.

- Vacancy Periods: Rental properties may experience periods without tenants, leading to lost income.
- Unforeseen Expenses: Maintenance, repairs, and unexpected costs can impact profitability.
- Regulatory and Legal Risks: Changes in property laws, zoning regulations, or tax policies can affect property ownership.
- Natural Disasters: Bushfires, floods, and other environmental risks can damage properties and impact their value.

Legislation Changes Risk

While some political parties and unions have suggested and promoted changes to negative Gearing a capital gains tax legislation there has been no Substantial changes in sight.

One of the smallest changes has been removal of claiming travel for rental investment properties. Additionally, there was some changes to depreciation laws which was outlined in the depreciation section earlier.

It is unknown what changes may be and how/what form they may take and whether they will be introduced if ever on a retrospective basis or forward basis. Historically they have only ever been introduced on a forward basis and not retrospective basis.

In my opinion with there being a housing shortage crisis at the moment, I do not believe that the government can possibly consider a major property tax reform at the moment. This would cause too much disruption to the property market crisis and shortage. However, there is some risk that there might be potential tax reforms making negative gearing non available or less attractive. If anything, this slight risk might be a reason to buy investment property earlier rather than later even more.

COMMON ERRORS PROPERTY OWNERS MAKE IN THEIR TAX

Here are some of the most common errors made by taxpayers:

- Can no longer claim travel to rental properties
- Expensing Assets immediately when they should be depreciated over time.
- Expensing Borrowing costs such as loan establishment fees and loan mortgage insurances immediately instead of amortising them over 5 years as a deduction.
- Omitting capital gains or not declaring rental income. Or reporting in the incorrect tax year. Capital gains accrue in the tax year of the sale of contract falls in rather than settlement date.
- Wrong calculations of capital gains, prorated capital gains or not adding back building depreciation from your depreciation report.
- Not Declaring a rental property in legal owner's tax return. Instead trying to put in another non-owner to pay less tax.
- You need to be GST registered and pay GST on sale of new residential property if you have developed the property with a view to make a profit considered a business by ATO. There needs to be GST adjustments with GST being repaid if property developers claim GST on purchases but then change purpose and not sell the construction as new residential home.
- Renting property at well below market value and not

declaring market value. ATO will deem you to rent at market value when not rented at arm's length party such as to family member.

- Loans must be directly related to an investment property to claim the interest cost. It must not include a home loan portion or loan components that were for private non-deductible purposes.

- Expenses for investment property can only be claimed when available for rent. Therefore, costs of building on holding before available for rent are either building Assets to be later depreciated or capital costs such as land holding costs that can offset a future capital gain.

- You cannot claim acquisition costs such as stamp duties or conveyancing costs as a deduction. But they are a capital acquisition cost that reduce capital gain when sold. The property in ACT is an exception to this.

- You cannot in general immediately expense Assets, however they can be depreciated over some years. Many investors misunderstand what qualifies as a repair or immediate deduction as against an improvement claimed over time. Using accelerated depreciation rates which are not as guided by ATO.

- Some investors miss their deductions including obtaining a depreciation report or claiming rates and taxes adjustments from their initial acquisition settlement or amounts from their rental agent annual statement. Some guess their loan interest amounts but as this is one of your biggest expenses claim you should get this spot on.

- Failing to keep records of deductions or of capital gains events including settlement statements, costs while living in property, or receipts of expenditures.
- Treating initial repairs as deductible. But repairs conducted before the property is rented are deemed capital works which must be claimed over time.
- Making errors on principal place of residence declarations to state bodies meaning incorrect land tax assessment are made leading to errors in land tax calculations and perhaps fines.
- Using the 5-year rule to avoid a capital gain at the same time as using a main residence exemption on another home property. You can only elect one main residence at any one time; you cannot span two over the same time.
- Trying to use the 5-year rule incorrectly when they property was not initially lived in as a home from the initial acquisition.
- Not correctly apportioning partly rented properties at a fair portion of rentable use, to reduce the rental profit.
- Not correctly apportioning the main residence days held out of a rental property sold which was lived in as a main residence and rented.
- Not understanding the tax treatment of different entities owning a property from individual, joint, company, trust and Self-Managed Super Fund (SMSF).
- Not complying with all the rules of owning a property by a Self-Managed Super Fund (SMSF) such as not renting to family members or using the

property. To own property with a Self-Managed Super Fund (SMSF), the property must be acquired and used solely for the purpose of providing retirement benefits. This means the property cannot be lived in or rented to a fund member or their related parties. Additionally, the SMSF cannot purchase the property from a related party, and any commercial lease to a related party's business must be at market rates.

Of course, with good accounting and tax agents you can comfortably comply with all the rules and regulations. In my opinion there is no need to take any risks and getting anything wrong in your tax or deliberately cheating is just simply not necessary. Just stick to the rules and make sure you and your advisors get things as right as possible to keep you out of trouble and keep happily enjoying your property ownership. Even when you pay all the legal tax you need to, you can still do well and thrive with your property ownership.

DIFFERENCES OF PROPERTY OWNERSHIP IN THE DIFFERENT OWNERSHIP ENTITIES EXPLAINED

To be a property investor, it is good to know how owning a property in different entity types can impact the tax treat and person your reasons to buy in a particular tax entity. We shall explain some of the differences in the tax entities and property ownership here.

Individual

The advantages of individually owning a property are simplicity for lending and borrowing. Able to access the benefits of negative gearing provided you have some solid income. You also have access to the 50% capital gain discount for assets sold after one year.

The main disadvantage is that there is least asset protection when owning property individually. This may pose more threat to high-risk professionals and self-employed persons.

There are fewer options for estate planning and no option to distribute property income to others.

Choosing an individual to own a property when a couple may be beneficial to choose the property profit distribution to the lower partner or property loss to the higher income earner. This may be more important too in times of extending the family and parenting breaks may reduce one partners income. In this case you may choose to negatively gear to the parent that remains working to utilise the deductions. This may have some lending complexities as both partners' income may be needed to get the loan that is owned by one spouse, but it may be tax beneficial to do so.

Joint

The advantages of jointly owning a property are simplicity for lending and greater borrowing capacity. Joint owners are both able to access the benefits of negative gearing provided you both have some solid income. You also have access to the 50% capital gain discount for assets sold after one year.

The main disadvantage is there is less asset protection when owning property jointly like individually. Again, this may pose more threat to high-risk professionals and self-employed persons.

There are some options for estate planning with the surviving partner inheriting a property and as income is distributed evenly to joint owners there is no option to distribute property income to others.

Choosing to jointly own a property when a couple may be beneficial to reduce some of the property profit distribution of a higher incomed partner to the lower partner. But unfortunately, may reduce a property loss to the higher income earner. So, when negatively geared it would be better for the higher income earner partner to get the deductions of negative gearing.

Disadvantage may occur when extending the family with parenting breaks mainly reduce one partners income. In this case when a partner has no income in parental leave, they may lose the benefit from negative gearing.

But for both individual and joint individual ownership, there are good benefits from the negative gearing to own one or two properties in this way. This will provided good tax benefits in their career. Post career if one or two properties are owned and owned outright some tax may be liable on this profit in post-retirement. However, it is more ideal to develop further wealth in other entities such as trust and Self-Managed Super Fund (SMSF). Owning one or two properties outright should not make for overly huge tax payable burden in retirement assuming to continue to hold the properties outright in retirement with passive income.

Companies

The advantages of owning a positively geared property in a company maybe be from the lower company tax rate of 25% for small businesses if individuals associated have high individual income already. As middle- and high-income earners individual tax rates are higher than this rate of 25%.

Another advantage is the additional asset protection of owning a property by a company.

However, it is not generally recommended to have property asset owned by business trading company, so as not to expose their business risk to valuable properties. In fact, some lenders will not lend to business trading companies.

Companies do not receive the 50% capital gain discount.

Negative gearing may not work in a company unless it has other income to offset the income to. This is because company losses cannot be utilised by other entities such as individuals.

Another reason to want to buy a property by a company may be to access retained earnings of a company to buy a property with. This is likely to be something to consider with your accountant or tax agent.

Set up costs are higher and there is an ongoing ASIC fee for companies in Australia, accounting compliance costs will also be higher.

Trusts

Negative gearing may not work in a Trust unless it has other income to offset the income to. This is because trust losses cannot be distributed to other entities such as individuals. This may make an investment property with negative profits not the right choice. This is because trust losses are trapped in the trust and can only offset future trust profits, which may only be capital gains often a long way away.

However, an investment property with a profit might be a good choice as the trust will enable distribution of the profit to a family member with less tax to pay such as an adult child going to higher education with low income or non-working spouse.

Trust may utilise the 50% Capital gain discount.

Set up costs are medium higher and there is an ongoing ASIC fee for companies in Australia, accounting compliance costs will also be higher. If trust is owned by a company complexity is higher than a company alone.

Trusts also offer good flexibility to estate plan property assets, as with the succession on individuals controlling the trust may simply pass to new controlling individuals, without changing property ownership.

Owning property in trusts for self-employed person can be a

great option. This is because they can acquire a negative geared property and distribute into the trust with a trust loss, against other income to utilise the losses from trading business income. This may be also a good way to protect assets for a self-employed person. It may also give good flexibility and cope with changes throughout a life and give optimal distribution to others ability up to retirement.

Self-Managed Super Fund (SMSF)

SMSF may have higher set up costs and ongoing compliance is high with annual audits require to demonstrate compliance for the concessional tax rates. They are highly complex with strict compliance laws there needs to be arm's length (to unrelated people such as sellers or tenants) transactions, the fund must benefit your retirement only, there are restrictions on private use of assets and funds cannot be accessed again until retirement and kept separate from personal funds.

Owning property in SMSF perhaps has the most tax benefits with the lowest tax rate of 15% pre-retirement and 0% after retiring.

SMSFs can borrow for property acquisition through limited recourse borrowing arrangements, these can be quite complex. They may add further to the high set up and compliance costs of SMSFs. However, they can be a quick and easy way to use funds in super as deposit to get another investment property.

Capital gains are calculated on an unrealised basis, which means a property when every few years will pay capital gain tax with only 33.3% (not 50%) discounted capital gains with the concessional rate of 15% before retirement.

SMSF can pool the funds of partner or families to get greater purchase property capacity. Members of SMSF have direct control over their investment choices and greater choices in hands on asset selections such as property. This maybe an excellent way to access your super funds to buy another property.

Owning property outright in SMSF with probable rental income profits, will likely snowball and accumulate your superannuation balances even faster along with consistent employer/extra super contributions will you to comfortable retirement super balances.

SMSF held in SMSF is protected from external creditor claims.

SMSF are subject to limits of currently 1.7m per members. Once one spouse has filed the SMSF limit they can work on their spouses.

Accumulating as much retirement wealth as possible in SMSF is a great idea to minimise post-retirement taxes. This is because superannuation is not taxed in the pension phase when retired. Having high wealth outside of Super may still leave you to pay high taxes on the investment income of these assets. So, try to focus more wealth in super for retirement.

Adding contributions to your super can also be tax deductible. Subject to limits and eligibility so check with your tax agent. But what a great thing to do add to your super investment and get a tax deduction for it.

WHAT DOES A BEAUTIFUL FINANCIAL FUTURE LOOK LIKE?

Have a good income

- Whether you are in business or working having an income is great. Or even passive income

- Find what you love to do whether that is a career or a business. If you love what you do it may improve your chances of earning a good income.

- What is an average income in Australia in 2025, $98000. However, set your own goal as to what you want to earn given your experience, qualifications, ability and confidence. If you are not currently happy with your income set a new income goal, give it a time frame and set some strategies on how to achieve it.

- Make plans and work towards your retirement income in your later years above 50.

Start investing

- It's not what you earn but what you save. Even with a huge income, you will not accumulate wealth unless you save and invest. It is more about what you save than earn.

- Make in what investment are for you such as buying property and shares.

- Set a saving and investing goal.

- What do you want to save each year? For how many years? I like $25000 per year for 20 years at 5% should get you to close to $1m at $826000. Pause for a moment to ponder this. Can you save this amount and stay on this simple plan to accumulate some savings like this. Can you stay committed and do this really simple task to save and invest yourself to getting there. Hopefully, I can quickly change your mindset that you can easily become a millionaire.

- Doing this and putting similar amounts into an investment property may be another way to do this. Also, I would be confident you will earn more than a return of 5% too. Or why not do this in your superannuation. Maybe do it inside and outside of superannuation.

Own/Owning a home

- Of course, start owning a home may be something you wish to do and as previously discussed. If you have work stability and know where you want to live it is a great idea to own your home. You can own it outright too or get there with the help of a loan. This is something you can do if you so desire.

Have a stash for a rainy day

- Always keep some money to enjoy your life

- Allow for children growing, medical, education and futures

- Keep some money in case sudden financial or medical change. Think about how much are you going to keep?

- How do you keep money for a rainy day? Bank accounts or loan offset accounts can be great way to do this. Some less liquid investments such as shares or term deposits can work too. Using a credit card may help if you can ideally pay it off by the payment due date.

Use negative gearing, it is what the rich do

- Sound familiar, you should know this if you have been reading this book.

- Ideally only one or two investment properties for hold with high debt levels. I am not saying to not own more properties but just not to have high debt investment properties of more than two properties. This helps your tax position with bigger refunds.

- Not only is the tax system encouraging this by giving you bigger refunds, your tenant is paying most of it for you and you are planting an investment tree which will add to your wealth.

Get behind your superannuation

- Super is blessed with a low tax rate of 15% before you retire and 0% tax on earnings after you retire.

- So, it is a great place to accumulate wealth whilst staying in a low tax environment.

- If you want to aim high and retire young, become a self-funding retiree with saving and super of $1m plus so you can retire at the age you desire. Follow the strategy I mention earlier of investing in superannuation $25000 for 20 to 25 years from about 40 to 50 to ensure you have an above $1000000 superannuation balance for retirement.

Plan for anything bad

- Have an updated will which your estate upon death and ensures your assets go to your chosen beneficiaries.

- Consider and review your personal insurances having private hospital cover, income protection insurances, property insurances over your cars, homes and investment properties. Having life insurances too to cover repaying large debt in case you die. Please not life insurance is generally not tax deductible. Income protection insurances generally are tax deductible. If outside of your superannuation fund they are an individual tax deduction. If inside your superannuation fund they are a deduction in your superannuation fund.

- Leave papers outlining your financial affairs in case anything happens to you. This may be an extensive exercise in complex financial affairs but vital to ensure assets are well succeeded and passed on. You wouldn't want to leave it lost and unknown about to your beneficiaries, would you? Leaving the keys and locks, mapping of all your financial affairs is both vital and responsible. You can also incorporate your funeral wishes into such a document. Ideally you could outline:

  - Current service providers such as phones, internet and utility providers.
  - Social media profiles and access for in case of death requests
  - Investments such as property managers, banks, cryptocurrency holdings, financial

investments holdings, share brokers and holdings.

- o Details of all insurances including most importantly life insurances.
- o Superannuation details. Keep beneficiary updated too.
- o Banking accounts and cards.
- o Anything else such as location of will or safe access.

- Protect your assets. This may include asset protection of you are self-employed. Having a clear succession plan for individual, superannuation, digital and business assets.

Lastly buy more fun stuff

If you have done all these, already try setting some more goals or enjoy spending some of your hard-earned wealth. Don't try to be the richest man in the cemetery is valuable advice. Leave some behind if you wish to beneficiaries but enjoy your assets most importantly while you are alive and well. Some ways to enjoy your wealth:

- Holiday houses and travel

- Fancy cars

- Donate

- No point in being the richest person in the graveyard, don't leave a huge estate behind by not spending and enjoying it or working way past a reasonable retirement age when you don't need to.

WHAT SHOULD SOME OF YOUR MAIN FINANCIAL OBJECTIVES BE AT DIFFERENT STAGES OF YOUR LIFE

It's good to know that at different stages of your life your financial goals and objectives may change depending on that stage of life.

Young

Generally, for younger investors that have more of an ability to tackle more risk with a focus on growth and they have got time on their side, and they can ride out market fluctuations for potentially higher gains. Their main priorities might be to increase income, establish their careers and families, also it is never too early to start investing. They may be pursuing sporting interests and travelling.

They should develop good financial habits early, build financial literacy, accumulate some savings, invest in bank accounts, shares or managed investments ETFs, understand and monitor their superannuation. Keep an emergency fund for covering ideally 6 months.

Commonly they may be buying a first car for personal or work purposes. Ideally not overspending on most expenses such as credit cards, phone and cars.

It can be a time of many jobs, so consolidate your superannuation into just one account, you could save money and fees and reduce paperwork.

Ideally some savings toward a first home is an exceptional start for a young person to achieve.

Young family Mid Life.

At this stage of life commonly relationships are building into families. Often there is more of a worth building objective with the focus on loan reduction such as education loans or home loans. Financial commitments begin to rise with increasing cost of living pressures, housing affordability and costs of raising a family such as education and childcare.

At this ager superannuation accumulation for the distant retirement is not yet a high priority. Over contributing to superannuation and locking funds in jail in your superannuation until you are 70 or so may be against other more important priorities such as having money as a deposit for a home, family raising or paying for the wedding.

Accomplishments at this stage in life would generally be around buying a home, getting into a serious relationship with a partner, raising children and paying down debt.

At this stage, you may also wish to diversify investment portfolios such as shares, real estate, and managed funds and set up funds or children such as educational friends. Risk appetite may vary greatly depending on your personal circumstances and views.

This is a perfect age to buy property investments home property investment or investment property to assist with wealth creation and negative giving tax benefits.

With young families and higher debt levels it is a good time to protect loved ones in the family with strengthened personal insurance is such as life insurance and income protection insurance. Nominating a beneficiary in your superannuation is vital and can save tax if not given to dependant's spouse or children.

If available consider salary sacrificing option in your work to save or tax too. Just be sure what the salary sacrificing option is such as a health worker can contribute to home loan repayments which is great. However, if the only option is to contribute to superannuation it may not yet be your priority to do.

Approaching retirement

This is a time to prioritise the wealth that they worked hard for and focus on income-generating ways to maintain their lifestyle and enjoy life style.

This is the age to start looking after your health more.

It is also quite time to begin to accumulate wealth in your superannuation and hopefully at time we debt levels have come down. Well then you might still be investing it may be a time to start weaning down the investment growth as you achieve a more comfortable position towards retirement. Typically, later in this stage you might be thinking about simplifying your financial affairs into a simpler retirement affordable position. A good rule of thumb is to invest in assets you can own for ten to fifteen years.

If your superannuation is doing well share more into your spouses in times of raising children.

Consider diversifying your investments between whatever you prefer as investment such as property, shares, ETFs, cryptocurrencies or precious metals. Or if you are not sure how to directly invest in these invest in ETF's that can be very specific such as crypto, Gold or AI shares.

Your net worth and estimated retirement position is of greater interest as you plan towards retirement. You may want to use a spreadsheet or Superannuation balance calculator to calculate your retirement superannuation balance position.

You may use less negative gearing and more superannuation strategies such as transition to retirement strategies. You would also be looking to maximise super contributions taking advantage of super contribution limits to boost your savings and maximise tax deductions.

It might be a time to fine-tune your superannuation in general as well and you may even consider an option such as a Self-Managed Super Fund (SMSF) or manage funds for your superannuation to safeguard your principle and investment.

Family may be more independent and older but there may still be some requirements to assist children such as helping them with first homes. The empty nest phase will give you more time and money to focus on yourself again.

It's never too early to start planning your retirement, I mean an idea of where your superannuation balance will get to and your wealth outside of superannuation can give you a good idea if you're on the right track. Additionally, some good financial planning advice can assist you with the mentioned maximum super contributions before you retire, when to retire, how much you can afford when you are retired and doing transition to retirement strategies prior to retirement.

Signs of being in a more comfortable financial free position my allow you to spend more freely an enjoyable thing in life such as more travel, new luxury cars or homes. It is a time to begin to choose life over work more.

It might be a time a windfall may come along from inheritances or redundancies. This can assist some lifestyle enjoyment or boost your investments or superannuation.

It can also be a time of considering a home downsize. This refers to a way of unlocking some wealth into more spendable retirement or lifestyle cash. This is by taking some of your home sold and buying another for less creating a profit and smaller place to live. Taking the downsize change, can increase up your retirement funds and this can also be put into your superannuation.

Retirees

Having just done a great job or working, getting into a retirement position with some good advice or decisions. It is a time to make big decisions about your future and finances. It can be hard to get this right, financial planning and pension application can be tricky to navigate alone.

You will need to reassess your investment strategy for your retirement, typically reducing your risks to much lower lowers than while working. You may have stopped working but your superannuation should be working hard still to provide you a strong and steady income to enjoy your retirement in.

You may apply for pension benefits or transition your superannuation until retirement phase. Which means you can no longer contribute to it, it becomes and you must draw down and minimum amount from your superannuation.

Obviously, retirement is a time to enjoy. Spend and run down your wealth while you can still be healthy. Remember not to become the richest man in the cemetery and enjoy your wealth and spend happily in your retirement.

If you run out of superannuation you can always try to get the pension.

CASES OF PROPERTY SUCCESS

Case One

Bob was considering selling a rental property.

He owned a home with a home loan debt that was larger than his investment home loan. He found out he could only claim the interest directly related to his investment home loan but wished he could take off more home loan. He knew about paying off the home loan first as it isn't tax deductible and had been paying a minimal amount on his investment home loan as it was tax deductible. But still he asked if there was a way to legally pay off the home loan.

Yes, to look at selling his investment property and use proceeds to repay the home loan.

He sought advice and was told the capital gain would be around $150,000 after applying the 50% discount.

He decided to take a year off work to reduce additional taxable income. In that tax year he was having the sabbatical, he sold the property as per plan.

Additionally, he made extra super contribution to super. Although his normal super contribution limit is $30,000 per year, his tax agent advised him he had some unused carry forward amount. So, he was able to do a tax-deductible super contribution of $70,000 reducing his taxable income to $80,000k and hence his tax bill was $18,000. If he had have continued to work, his usual salary of $150,000 and with no super contributions his taxable income would have been $300,000 which would have been taxed at $112,000. So, he saved around $100,000 in tax. Sure, he may have forgone $150,000 in salary, but he travelled and really enjoyed the year off too.

He took the $500,000 after tax he got from selling the house and repaid his home loan in full very satisfyingly.

He is now approaching the bank as he now has 100% equity in his home and back to work and will by another investment property. That loan being fully tax-deductible and with no non-deductible home loan anymore.

So, in this case we should you how you can switch down your home loan from a lower investment home loan balance situation.

Case Two

Wendy and Jimmy were in their fifties and had a stable income without a lot of deductions.

I encouraged them to buy an investment property.

They were also worried about their children ever being able to afford their own homes.

They sought a loan and found a property in Adelaide. They said it was highly competitive to find the property but eventually did. Although they thought they would be able to buy more for the loan approval amount they eventually bought what they could a bedroom or two smaller. All they needed to do to get the loan was prove their incomes and show they owned a lot of equity in their home.

They did their first tax return post the rental property and both zoomed up to get a tax refunds of $4k each, which they have never gotten before. Previously they barely got 1k in tax refunds.

They are also delighted that in three years their property price has gained more than 250k. This is making them feel more comfortable about paying off their home loan faster and that they will before retiring. The property is also an option for their kids to live in later. They were very happy they decided to buy an investment property. They simply needed to show their income was good and home equity position to get a loan and then chase down a nice property.

Case Three

Jason is a young professional who has saved well and earns high bank interest, so he was typically has to pay tax on his tax return from the high interest earned.

After buying a property he thought about living in it, but his parents welcomed him to stay at home longer. So, he rented out the property but would like to live there later when he is ready or perhaps when a partner comes along.

He impressed the bank which his professional income and savings in the bank as a deposit. It was even more affordable when he decided not to live in it as the investment home loan amount approved was higher than a home loan.

When he did his tax return, he also did a tax depreciation report meaning he could claim an extra 10k deduction per year to add to his negative gearing position. He didn't immediately know this until advised.

So, since his last tax return, which was $2k payable with the bank interest, the bank interest has gone as he used the money in the bank to buy his property. The negative profit of the investment property has changed his tax return outcome to a refund of $9k. He is delighted about the refund and relieved he got a property before they increased further.

Case Four

Jennifer was in a great financial position but came across an opportunity to buy a property adjacent to his vacant land. Which she wanted to do a property development on.

She was able to get a loan to buy the property which he had to use her properties as equity for the loan.

To obtain a construction loan, she had to own both land sites outright, which she financed to other properties she had.

She then with a builder, built townhouses on the properties which were owned by a trust and registered for GST meaning she claimed GST on the Construction costs as she planned to subdivide and build the townhouses for profit.

When completed her bank asked her to sell some of the properties which she did for profit and declared this as income and paid GST on the sale of the property under margin scheme. This means the land value of the sale price came off. A simple example is if we sell for 620k and the land value is 400k the GST on sale is (620-400)/11 which is $22,000. As she decided to keep the rest of the properties, she repaid the GST claimed in construction.

She now has a big loan, but this is manageable by the tenants she has paying her good rents. Her losses from the negative gearing from the townhouses can be utilised by the business income she has. The assets are away from her personal asset pool which reduced her professional risks as a lawyer. Her bank has access to her properties for security and she has optimised lending arrangement for future investments.

She is glad she did it, recognising the land she bought is now increased $500,000 since 2020, and her townhouse have all risen $250,000 each since being built two years ago. It may be good timing as the property markets have been escalating but at the same time was not an easy ride in the park to do.

She is looking forward to one day whittling down the big loan and possibly owning them outright in retirement or they offer options such as something for the kids or even a downsize option for her. Anyway, she has time to pay off the loan with about 15 years of work she loves still to go. In the meantime, she is proud she has done it as one of her best financial moves of her life.

She also has bought property in her SMSF and keenly adds the $30,000 super contribution to her super each year. This helps reduce her business taxes and accumulates her wealth in super faster as she already owns property outside of super too. She has bought property in other states to keep her land tax done as hers is high in South Australia. Her outright property owned is providing more super accumulation; she bought this which her old employee days super accumulated. She has also bought a property in Melbourne as she thinks it is good value and a cheaper property market in Australia. On this property she took out a limited recourse borrowing arrangement. Describing the banking process as more difficult but worth it. Her quick property tip to me was, don't go on holiday while a property is settling if you want to have a peaceful holiday.

FINAL THOUGHTS SUMMARIZED ON WHY TO BUY PROPERTY

Buying property leverages resources well to help you create wealth that includes your tenant paying for most of it, using other people's money your banks to finance it and other expert advisors to improve your gains such as your property advisors, accountants, financial advisors, bankers, finance brokers, tax depreciation reporting, property managers and conveyancers. Of course, property leverages time to make your increased net worth by compounding growth.

Owning property in Australia is tax-efficient. Our tax system subsidises your investment property when negatively geared. So, when you have little or no deductions either as an employee or self-employed, investment properties will help you get bigger tax deductions and therefore bigger refunds.

Investment property can give you bigger tax refunds that can add thousands to your tax return each year. This might up add up to hundreds of thousands in your working career. That's a lot of tax savings and helps your net worth grow.

If you buy a home property this is also a great investment that makes money too. Although costs of holding are not a tax deduction, it is still tax beneficial because it is exempt from capital gains tax as your home has a main residence exemption to this tax. This also gives you stability and the pride of owning your own home.

Owning investment property can improve you from minor to major tax deductions with the negative gearing deductions. So, if you are on a high income with only a few deductions or even if you just want more deductions, having an investment property can quickly increase your deductions and therefore your tax refund. This amount depends on the numbers of your rental property such as rental income and expenses, loan amounts, interest paid, depreciation and other taxable income levels and the year affected tax rates.

For people struggling to afford to buy a home property, why not buy an investment property which is more affordable as the tenant pays for most of it, you get tax deductions and bigger refunds. Then wait for capital gains which can fasten your ambitions to buy a home.

Property investing makes big capital gains on net wealth gains from owning homes and investment properties. I believe wealth creation is active and difficult from employment or business sources compared to passive income from property investment ownership.

Owing property can gain the capital gains to fund equity contributions to catapult you to buy further property purchases, accelerating your net worth.

There is a high return on your time. Earnings per hour are better than hourly rates at your employment or self-employment. Time returned on investing in property for small hours can make thousands of dollars of return per hour of effort. This is much more than what your work or business pays you per hour.

In the past decade, from 2015 to 2025, has seen median house prices more than double in several cities in Australia, showing the mighty power of long-term capital growth in property investment as a wealth-building tool.

Forced savings is a key benefit to owning property. Financial disciplining you to invest and perhaps saving on unnecessary expenditure. It can motivate you to repay loans faster by adding more to your loan repayments, saving more interest and adding to your net worth.

Property is in a state of price escalation. In my experience and it is also historically shown that some properties double in 10 to 20 years making more than half a million dollars. Property investment remains one of the best ways to accumulate wealth in Australia. Historical price escalations in property make it very worthwhile.

Some factors outlined in this book indicate this Price escalation may continue. This includes increasing land costs and shortage of land, increasing building times and increasing costs of building labour and materials.

High costs of buying and selling property make it smart to hold the property for a longer term. This better absorbs the buying and selling costs. Along with the tax efficiencies and potential for capital growth, it makes property investment a smart thing to do. Holding properties is like letting your trees grow. The best time to plant an investment property is ten years ago but the second-best time to plant a property investment is now.

Avoid the biggest property investment remorse of selling your property too early. Then seeing it rise steeply when you no longer own it. Keep property unless you must sell it for financial reasons or you are simplifying your wealth position in your later career.

Let your Assets earn money for you rather than just selling your time in employment or business. Not only now but in the future too.

Loans on your properties with hard work can inevitably be paid off. This leaves you with excellent passive income and positive cash flow which can support your pre- or post-retirement income. Owning properties outright later in life give you options like using them as a downsized home, letting children/family use or even making it a holiday house. This can appease your worry about your kids and how they are going to get a home one day in this modern world with escalating housing prices.

Currently, low interest rates mean you may be able to invest further and gain greater returns Outperforming your low interest rates. This may sound difficult but remember that in some cities property values doubled in the last 10 years from 2015 to 2025.

Demand for rental properties remains strong leading to increased rents and rental yields with low vacancy rates.

 The property has investment potential and has historically been a stable property market in Australia.

Purchasing property with the right advice in the right legal structure and in the correct personal circumstances can be a very successful financial strategy in Australia.

SO, YOU WANT TO BUY A PROPERTY – HOW TO DO IT?

AT A GLANCE

Here is a snapshot of what to do to get your property:

I often say, see what you can borrow, so chase the loan first.

Then get advice from your accountant on how to own the property and know all the tax implications and any other guidance they may offer. Book here to for property tax advice with me.

Begin speaking to Property agents and researching online listings, find out what and where you can buy.

When you find something of interest, dive at the property as it is a tough competition buyer market now. In particular in some states such as South Australia, but Victoria being less competitive.

If you find a property, engage a conveyancer and carry out the settlement.

If it is an investment property, get it rented as soon as possible with a Rental property manager.

Continue to comply with Tax obligations with your tax agent and follow through with advice such as obtaining a tax depreciation report and including rental property income and expenses in your tax returns.

Apply for your depreciation report

Book in for your rental property tax return here.

Stay in touch with the value of your property, not every day but every few years,

Once you get that property and everything is under control, reset your goals. Perhaps consider investing more.

STEP BY STEP

Buying property in Australia is an exciting journey, but it requires careful planning. Here's a step-by-step guide to get started:

- Assess Your Financial Situation – Determine your budget, savings, and borrowing capacity. A mortgage broker or lender can help clarify your options. Knowing all the figures on your current goals and incomes is a great foundation to start with. Knowing the family income, having an idea of what sort of property you wish to buy, is it investment or a home. Will you build or buy an existing? What savings and resources do you have to contribute to the purchase?

- Obtain Loan Pre-Approval – One of the first important steps, unless you have enough to buy the property outright, is to see if lenders will support you to buy a property. They will gain information on your financial position to meet their lending criteria, including deposit/security and loan repayment capacity. Securing pre-approval from a lender shows sellers you're serious and helps you set a realistic price range. Once you are told you have an approval in place, you basically have a budget for how much you can buy a property for.

- Research the Market – Explore different locations, property types, and price trends to find an area that suits your needs. I suggest narrowing down your prospective area to buy in. The less are the better. Even narrow it down to a suburb such as Hurstville

NSW 2220. They you can quickly get to speed on the value of that suburb and get notifications on recent sales in the area. You may even start to know the value of similar properties. Some where you know and are familiar with is a great place to start, for instance some suburb you enjoyed living in previously.

Some of the most important details you may need:

For owner occupying Homes

- Title type such as separate tile or strata/community.
- Rates - council, water, strata
- Age of building
- Builder
- House Plans
- Do you love this property and want to live here. Are the size, location, and features to your liking. Are the local area and facilities to your liking.

For investment properties

- Title type such as separate tile or strata/community.
- Rates - council, water, strata
- Get a rental per week appraisal, verify this with another agent
- Age of building
- Keep a track of all the properties you are considering, it is easy to lose track of which properties are which after a while.

Property tracking and analysis

I suggest this sort of table to keep, to track you cashflow

estimates and rental yields, this might help you see which properties are the winners. Also keep your property listing link handy, you may need to use it often.

Property Link	Https://Www.Realestate.Com.Au/Xxxxx
Agent	Xxxx Xxxxx
Property	Xxxxxxx, Suburbville State NNNN
Suburb	XXXXX
Year Build	Xxxx
Beds Bath Cars	1,1,1
Cost	610-640
Offer	625000
Rent	725pw
Rent Pa	37700
Water	700
Council	1684
Strata	3600
Interest	37500
Agent	3317.6
Other	5000
Net Loss	-14101.6
Dept	7812.5
	-21914.1
Refund	-10299.627
	-11614.473
Comments	
Rental Yield	6.03
Net Rental Yield	5.07
Outcome	Make An Offer

If you are buying interstate do be afraid to ask for a virtual show through.

Know a little about the offer and cooling-off process in the state you are making an offer in. For instance, in NSW there is a small deposit made which you lose if you pull out of the contract while doing your due diligence on the property within the cooling-off period of days. This is good to know so you are not wasting the deposit signing a contract too early. Your conveyancer can guide you on this too.

If necessary, get strata reports and building inspection reports. Don't skimp on these as they may save your thousands of dollars. You want to make the right decision in your purchase.

If you can get access to property reports, consider doing so too. Your local real estate agent not selling the property may be able to assist you to do or previous real estate agents you have used.

Engage a Conveyancer – Consider hiring a solicitor or conveyancer to guide you through legal aspects and checking contracts. They will confirm the stamp duties and conveyancing costs at settling, buying your property and be on your side to protect you from anything going wrong in the settlement process. A conveyancer plays a crucial role in the legal and administrative process of buying property in Australia.

The Role of a Conveyancer:

- Reviewing Contracts – They examine the contract of sale and advise you on any concerns or risks before you commit.

- Handling Legal Documents – They prepare, certify, and lodge essential paperwork, such as the contract of sale and transfer of land documents.

- Conducting Property Searches – They check for outstanding debts, zoning regulations, and any government interests in the property, such as planned developments.

- Managing Financial Transactions – They hold deposit money in a trust account and ensure payments like stamp duty and other rates are correctly processed.

- Ensuring Compliance – They verify your identity and ensure all legal requirements are met for a smooth settlement.

- Coordinating Settlement – They liaise with banks, sellers, and other parties to finalize the property transfer and ensure everything is legally binding.

- A conveyancer helps protect your interests and ensures the transaction is legally sound.

Seek Tax Advice

Getting tax advice when buying property in Australia is essential because it helps you navigate complex tax laws and avoid costly mistakes. Here's why it matters:

- Stamp Duty Costs – Each state has different stamp duty rates, and exemptions may apply for First-Home Buyers or investors.

- Advice you on the best way to structure the

ownership of the property

- Capital Gains Tax (CGT): Explain to you any capital gains tax implications.

- If you are property developing, you need tax advice for the correct business structure to minimize tax, GST implications and to know your numbers through the property development process.

- Tax Deductions – your tax agent should be proactive in guiding your investment property deductions, allowing for deductions for expenses like mortgage interest, maintenance, and depreciation.

- GST Considerations – Some property purchases, like new developments, may include GST, affecting your overall costs.

- Foreign Investor Taxes – If you're a non-resident, additional taxes and restrictions may apply.

A tax advisor ensures you maximize benefits while staying compliant with Australian tax laws.

Book in for your property tax advice session at https://bit.ly/4oNQ5Nb. More information at Property Accountant Adelaide | Tax Accounting Adelaide or Expert tax Adelaide | Tax Accounting Adelaide.

The Buying Process in Practice

- Start House Hunting – Attend open inspections, compare properties, and negotiate with sellers. Start checking out properties, existing or new if building, look at building display homes.

- Make an Offer & Sign Contracts – Once you find the right property, negotiate the price and sign a contract with conditions that protect you. There is a shortage of good value properties, so when you find one, you need to dive into the property. Don't let it slip by for a small amount of thousands because getting the property and making the capital gains should surpass the haggling savings when you are making an offer.

- Complete Settlement – Your solicitor will handle the final paperwork, ensuring a smooth transfer of ownership.

The Value of Professional Advisors

When buying property in Australia, having the right advisors can make a huge difference. Here are some key experts to consider:

- Buyer's Agents – They help you find and negotiate the best property deals, ensuring you don't overpay. These

- Property Investment Advisors – They provide strategic guidance on market trends, investment opportunities, and long-term planning. They provide value if you do not know where you want to buy, and can give you researched better-value properties.

- Accountants & Financial Planners – They assist with tax planning, budgeting, and structuring your finances for property investment.

- Real Estate Agents – They offer insights into local markets and help facilitate property transactions.

- Property managers – They help you get better quality tenants, look after your maintenance on your property, collect your rent, gain greatest rental possible and keep you up to date with your investment property compliance.

- Lawyers & Conveyancers – They ensure all legal aspects of the purchase are handled correctly, including contracts and title transfers. If you are building, a good lawyer can protect you from your building company.

- Property Valuers – They assess the true market value of a property to prevent overpaying.

- Insurance Brokers – They help secure appropriate property insurance to protect your investment.

- Quantity Surveyors – They provide depreciation schedules, which can help maximize tax benefits for investors.

Each expert plays a unique role in ensuring a smooth and successful property purchase.

We'll help you secure the right investment loan for your specific needs. If you're ready to explore your property investment options, contact us today!

READY TO BUILD WEALTH THROUGH PROPERTY INVESTMENT?

Need more advice and assistance to get to you there.

TAKE THE FIRST STEP

Take the first step toward financial freedom with the team that's helped hundreds of clients create wealth through strategic property investment.

BOOK YOUR PROPERTY INVESTMENT STRATEGY SESSION

- 60-minute personalised consultation
- Review of your current financial position
- Customised property investment roadmap
- Tax optimisation strategies for property investors

TAKE ACTION NOW – DON'T MISS THE OPPORTUNITY

PROPERTY TAX ADVICE BOOKING LINK

https://outlook.office.com/owa/calendar/TaxAccounting Adelaide2@taxaccountingadelaide.com/bookings/s/wM

<u>**W47Y8h0UKos8lAEwjrSg2**</u>

*"I've helped hundreds of Australians build wealth through property. Let me show you how the right tax and investment strategy can transform your financial future." - **Romeo Caporaso***

FOR A MORE ACTION-FOCUSED APPROACH:

TAKE ACTION NOW: DON'T MISS THE PROPERTY OPPORTUNITY

Book in for your property <u>tax advice session</u> at <u>https://bit.ly/4oNQ5Nb</u>. More information at <u>Property Accountant Adelaide | Tax Accounting Adelaide</u> or <u>Expert tax Adelaide | Tax Accounting Adelaide</u>.

Property values continue to rise while you're deciding. Book your no-obligation Property Wealth Blueprint Session and discover:

- How much property can you afford right now
- The tax advantages available specifically for your situation
- Which Adelaide suburbs offer the best investment potential
- How to structure your investment for maximum tax efficiency

CONNECT WITH ME

Welcome! I'd love to stay connected. Follow me on social media and reach out anytime!

Social Media

Stay updated and engage with me on these platforms:

- **Instagram**: https://www.instagram.com/taxaccountingadelaide/#

- **Twitter**: https://x.com/taxaccountingsa

- **Facebook**: https://www.facebook.com/TaxAgentAdelaide

- **LinkedIn Business**: https://www.linkedin.com/company/tax-accounting-adelaide/

- **LinkedIn Professional:** https://www.linkedin.com/in/romeocaporaso/recent-activity/all/

- **YouTube:** https://www.youtube.com/@TaxAccountingAdelaid

- **TikTok:** https://www.tiktok.com/@taxaccountingadelaide

Contact

https://www.taxaccountingadelaide.com/.

Let's Connect

I love engaging with my community! Feel free to leave a comment, send a message, or just say hi.

I would love to hear from you on your Property history or if my book has helped you on your property journey.

REFERENCES

- Australian Bureau of Statistics. (2025). *Housing demand and population trends*. Retrieved from https://www.abs.gov.au
- CoreLogic. (2025). *Home Value Index Report: June 2025*. Retrieved from https://www.corelogic.com.au
- Parliament of Australia. (2025). *Housing affordability in Australia: Current challenges and policy responses*. Retrieved from https://www.aph.gov.au
- PwC. (2025). *Emerging trends in real estate Australia 2025*. Retrieved from https://www.pwc.com.au
- Reserve Bank of Australia. (2024). *Statement on monetary policy*. Retrieved from https://www.rba.gov.au

Note on legislation and tax rates

Tax rates, thresholds, and legislative references in this book are current at the time of publication. Laws and regulations may change. Readers should verify information with the Australian Taxation Office (ATO) or seek independent professional advice relevant to their circumstances.

* 9 7 9 8 9 0 1 8 1 0 5 9 0 *